H. Thomas

D1491891

H. H. A. : LETTERS TO A FRIEND
Second Series - - 1922—1927

Photo: Drummond Young, Edinburgh.

LORD OXFORD

H. H. A.

LETTERS OF THE EARL OF OXFORD AND ASQUITH TO A FRIEND

Second Series
1922—1927

GEOFFREY BLES
TWO MANCHESTER SQUARE
LONDON, W.1

PRINTED AND MADE BY
HAZELL, WATSON AND
VINEY LIMITED
LONDON AND
AYLESBURY

First published June 1934

INTRODUCTION

THE First Series of these letters ranged from June 13th, 1915, to March 15th, 1922, and of these only eight were written while Mr. Asquith was still Prime Minister. These eight letters contained only two or three references to politics, and those of a personal nature. He mentioned, for instance, the difficulty he had had in bracing himself to propose a Vote of Credit in the House of Commons following the news of Raymond Asquith's death at the front. " I got on," he wrote on October 11th, 1916, " rather better than I expected, as everyone was very kind and sympathetic " ; and those who look up that speech will find that it was a triumph over personal emotions. In the letter written after his resignation, he said, " I saw I could not go on without dishonour or impotence, or both ; and nothing could have been worse for the country and the war " ; and he added that it was a relief to be rid of " the daily stream of boxes and telegrams : not to mention Cabinets and Committees and colleagues, etc." Here he was expressing what he felt, or part of what he was feeling—at the moment. He never believed that the direction of affairs then passed into better hands.

INTRODUCTION

After his resignation, when he was writing as one who could only influence decisions indirectly, if at all, his references to politics and political leaders became more frequent and more frank. He had, so invariably, kept his personal feelings apart from politics that it came as a surprise to some of his admirers, and as a relief to some of his opponents, to discover that his private letters did not exhibit the same imperturbable magnanimity as his public utterances; as though the proof of that did not lie in the contrast between what he might think as a man and see fit to act upon or express in public. The interest of this continuation of his letters to the same correspondent is still, therefore, biographical rather than historical. In them we can follow the preoccupations of his leisure, and his reflections at important junctures such as the General Strike.

Yet, in the main, allusions of a more personal character preponderate in these later letters; they deal with books read, plays visited, and people or pictures seen—subjects in which he and his correspondent Mrs. Harrisson had discovered a common interest in the early days of their friendship. This dated from February 1915, when they first met while Mr. Asquith was staying with his sister-in-law, Mrs. Graham Smith, at Easton Grey, near Malmesbury.

Afterwards she was often a guest at The Wharf, and later she lived on Boar's Hill, which was not many miles away.

Some of the letters in this Second Series narrowly escaped destruction. When Lord Oxford was writing his *Memories and Reflections* he found many of the letters in this series useful in helping him to recall past details, for he had kept no diary. Thinking of them only in that connection, he tore some of them across, as was his habit when a note or document had served its immediate purpose, instead of returning them with the bulk of the correspondence. These particular letters, although portions of them have appeared in his *Memories and Reflections* (my thanks are due to Messrs. Cassell for permission to reprint them), contain matter of equal interest which would have been lost had not Lady Oxford gathered them together, and, realising they must be precious to Mrs. Harrisson, returned them to her.

The Second Series extends up to the date of Lord Oxford's last illness. In the latest letters will be found some references to the symptoms which foreshadowed his death, and the end of a long and intimate friendship which had brought him much happiness.

DESMOND MACCARTHY.

April 1934.

H. H. A. : LETTERS TO A FRIEND
Second Series - - 1922—1927

44 Bedford Square, W.C.,

21st March, 1922.

I am glad that you have found a haven for Jumbo, where he will no longer be tempted to worry sheep.

Some letters of Margot's which had been the rounds of Lucy, etc., arrived this morning. She had had rather a fiasco at Pittsburg : thanks to the reporters having published a lying statement that she had said that the " American female is a painted plaything," a large Club of women cancelled their seats, and she had an audience of 12,000 instead of 15,000. It is, as she says, a Press-ridden country—and such a Press ! She was going on South and West to places like Cincinnati and St. Louis : terrible distances.

The Oxford Book of Italian Verse was an appropriate peace-offering from the peccant and taciturn R. H. I have dipped into it occasionally, but apart from Dante, who stands by himself, I can get very little out of Italian poetry.

This is a rather good compositor's mistake, which may amuse you. It ends a description of a Revivalist meeting : " The meeting then broke up, but a large *crow* (crowd) remained on the platform and sang

II.—B   I

lustily ' Rock of Ages ' for two hours." It equals my favourite : " In order to love, il faut sortir *le soir* " (de soi).

I thought we might on Sunday drive first to Stratford and get Corelli to give us lunch, and then push on into Worcestershire. If this seems to you a good plan, you might perhaps send her a line, as I shall be away Thursday and Friday in Scotland. I shall be back here to breakfast Saturday morning and drive down to The Wharf. It is snowing here to-day.

I hope you will get Pompey [1] to-morrow. I told them to send you also Chesterton's *Eugenics and other Evils*, which I think will probably amuse you.

Before lunch I looked in for a few minutes at the Goupil Gallery to sample their little Exhibition, which is well worth seeing when you come up next week. I enclose the Catalogue ; you will see that there is one drawing by James Pryde : quite interesting. There is a beautiful Wilson Steer. I was the only visitor except a hobbling old man in rusty, shabby black. My friend asked me if I would like to be introduced to him ; it was Walter Graves—whose Hammersmith Bridge, painted when he was 16, has just been bought by the Chantrey Trustees. There are several things by him at the Goupil, one quite a fine landscape. I, of

[1] Masefield's *Pompey the Great*.

2

course, said Yes, and had some talk with the old man, who after a time shambled away. When he was gone I asked how old he was.

" Over 80."

" What of his black hair and moustache ; dyed, I suppose ? "

" No, he cannot afford to have hair-dye ; we believe that he just puts his hand up the chimney to get a coating of soot which he transfers to his head."

I wish you had been there to see him. He was for many years Whistler's " devil," and used to be accused of palming off his own works as Whistler's. Many of his best, however, were done before he knew W., and the critics all now agree that he has a touch of genius of his own. But he is too old to paint and has nothing left to sell. Isn't it a tragic story ?

44 BEDFORD SQUARE, W.C.,

28th April, 1922.

I hope you had a good run of Madame Tussaud. I had a dull time at the House.

I went this morning with Elizabeth to the Private View at the Academy, a dismal collection of mediocre daubs. The only good picture in the whole Exhibition is by Connard—an interior with a quarrelling husband and wife—well-named " Why ? " There are two portraits—one by Sargent—of Lady Rocksavage, who, one would have thought, would be a good model : both quite bad. We soon had enough of this, and went on before lunch to the Grafton Gallery, where, among the usual McEvoys, etc., there were three things of James Pryde, all quite remarkable, and one, " The Slum " (apparently in an Italian town), of first-rate quality. I should have liked to be rich enough to buy it, but that would have made no difference, for we found, on looking at the price book, that it was not for sale. No doubt it will fall into the maw of Lady Cowdray.

I have had Elizabeth and " Dr. Clifford " [1] and Beb to lunch, with a quite clever American journalist called Hunt. He talked well about the position of negroes and Jews in the United States.

Elizabeth and I are just about to motor to The Wharf. I am coming to you to-morrow Saturday morning. I will drop for the moment into the Seger dialect. *Domani voglio salire fino al monticello dei porchi, portando meco il quadro del celebre pittore F—s, e il libro bellissime illustrato, degli Uccelli.* I hope this is both clear and grammatical.

Blessings, etc.

---

[1] Clifford Sharp, editor of *The New Statesman.*

THE HOUSE OF COMMONS, S.W.1,

14th June, 1922.

I found an unexpectedly good gathering at dinner at " The Club " last night : A. J. Balfour, Haldane, Bishop Gore, Kenyon (of the British Museum), and a strange figure whom I have not encountered for years—Lord Tennyson, eldest son of the poet, and father to Clare's Lionel. He was the first Governor of the Commonwealth of Australia, and has a curious slightly abbreviated reproduction of his Father's magnificent head—on the whole the finest I have ever seen, not excluding Mr. Gladstone's. We had some very good talk—largely about Ireland and books. Someone said that the author of *If Winter Comes* had netted here and in America at least £50,000 : which I don't believe, but if it was half as much, it is a wonderful achievement for a writer of unsuccessful novels.

Did you see in *The Times* Birrell's review of Jane Austen's newly discovered schoolroom efforts ? They are really poor stuff, in the burlesque vein, but with a lot of promise.

Margot arrived at lunch time from Easton Grey : Lucy is following by motor, but as our stairs are prohibitive to her, she is staying with Diana Capel.

I set to work this morning on my article for *John Bull*, and I think it will be all right, with perhaps one or two good sentences.

Bongie and Maud Tree lunched with us. Violet came back from Paris last night (*not* by air), and went this morning to Munstead to the "quiet country wedding" of Barbara McLaren to Freyberg. Bongie reports that both my daughters resent the suggestion in my letter to *The Times*—founded on their own— that they are so fallible physically as to be sea-sick in the air.

I read quite a lot of *Antigone* before I went to bed last night : I hope you are doing the same.

The House is a desert of dullness to-night. Do you like Cobbett's description of Mr. Pitt as an orator, a "loud snorting bawler" ?

We are going to-morrow night to see Gladys Cooper in *The Second Mrs. Tanqueray*. I come to The Wharf on Friday and hope you can dine before *Major Barbara*.

44 BEDFORD SQUARE, W.C.,

15th June, 1922.

I am rather exhausted, for I have just finished my 1,500 words of the *John Bull* article, and dictated them to a young woman who came from the office. It doesn't, I believe, come out till Wednesday in next week, but they "go to Press" to-morrow.

They have sent me to-day two tickets for the Bradfield *Antigone* on Saturday, the 24th, very correct in form—Κερκὶς Ε βάθρον ξ—can you translate that? I think I must ask for two more : tho' I would much rather go *à deux*.

Margot went out to dinner last night to Ava Ribblesdale's. The result was that I had here Donald Somervell, E. Blackwell, and Satterthwaite. We played three rubbers of bridge and were quite happy. I was writing my article this morning until lunch, where we had Violet (just returned from Paris), Oc, and Eric Drummond, whom I was very glad to see for the first time for two years. He was my *best* Private Secretary through all the troubled times of 1911–1914, and is now Secretary-General of the League of Nations at Geneva, with a salary of about £7,000 a year. He came very opportunely to-day, for I was able to read to him my article, and get his criticisms upon it. I often miss him : never was there a more efficient or devoted and affectionate helper.

I must close this now.

Blessings.

44 BEDFORD SQUARE, W.C.,

27th June, 1922.

I had a solitary dinner last night, and went through the play, the *Antigone*, more or less carefully, and made some notes, and I hope to-night (I have given up going to the play) I may put them more or less into shape. I had a letter to-day from one Lewis (who is a cousin of Sir George and was in their business), which enclosed the photograph I have sent you of the scene just after Hæmon's " shrouded corpse " comes in. All through the wonderful dialogue between Creon and Hæmon, H. argues much more as a democrat against a despot than as a lover pleading for the life of his betrothed. My correspondent says that one of the Bradfield boys translated Πόλις γὰρ οὐκ ἔσθ' ἥτις ἀνδρὸς ἔσθ' ἑνός—" A State which is for One is State for None," which is not a bad rendering.

I went this morning to our little conclave at Lord Cowdray's. Those present were E. Grey, R. Cecil, D. Maclean, H. Gladstone, Cowdray and Crewe. We had quite a good talk. Winston at the end of his speech yesterday threatened the new Irish Government with coercion by British troops if they did not behave themselves : a bid (as most people interpreted

8

it) for Diehard support. Bonar Law at once saw this, and went one better : he has more hold than anybody upon the whole body of Conservatives—Diehard or otherwise. L. G. tried to out-trump them both ; but as he is now orientating definitely in the Liberal direction, implied that if the Treaty in Ireland broke down, and force had to be applied, it must be by " other hands " than his. Bob Cecil and Grey both construe this as meaning that he is personally riding for a fall, and anxious to find a pretext for an early resignation, when he will leave his Tory colleagues, reinforced by Winston, to " carry the baby," and declare himself a Liberal of Liberals. It is quite possible, and with our short-memoried rank and file, it may be a shrewd calculation. Meanwhile there is quite a storm brewing over the grant of Peerages and other Honours to millionaires, who pay for them by huge contributions to the party chest.

I go to Paisley by the night train to-morrow, Wed., and return Thursday night and shall be back in Bed. Sq. for breakfast on Friday. I am going to the " Gaudy " in Balliol Hall on Friday evening. Is there any chance of golf on Saturday ? I must close now as I want to hear E. Grey speak on Genoa in the House of Lords.

9

44 BEDFORD SQUARE, W.C.,

7th July, 1922.

Were you really in London yesterday and gave me no sign? This Graves adventure [1] was, of course, conceived in folly, and carried out under unforeseeably bad conditions. But I could hardly have believed that Mamma would not have taken in the poor innocent wayfaring waifs.

You don't throw any light on to-morrow. As at present advised, I shall drive down to The Wharf in time for lunch. I am bringing with me a draft MS. by Pringle for my Keynes article, which I ought to deliver complete on Tuesday.

I am glad you liked my Carducci translation : I think it must be right ; your alternative (which is really more grammatical) makes the situation ridiculous.

Our dinner at the Garrick last night turned out better than I feared. My fellow guests were R.

[1] Nancy and Robert Graves, the poet, were on their way across the downs to Brighton to pay her father a visit. Their equipage was a small covered-wagon drawn by a lean horse. The rain came down in torrents as they left Islip (their home): Boar's Hill was the first stage of the journey.

McKenna, two Anglo-Indian officials here on fur-
lough, one Plank, a young artist who does the cover
and the illustrations of *Vogue*, and A. J. Munnings. The
last named saved the situation. After he had been
slightly—not immoderately—primed by wine, he re-
cited two ballads (one of enormous and the other of
considerable length) on hunting and steeple-chasing
and other forms of country sport. I thought that they
were unpublished works of Jan : they were quite up to
his best achievements in that peculiar genre. It turned
out that as a matter of fact they were Munnings' own :
they certainly ought to be published—partly because
he knows far more intimately than Masefield the
actual technique of the stable and the race-course.
He delivered them with marvellous *brio*. He and his
wife (a very nice woman) came here to-day by a pure
accident to lunch, with the Mastermen,[1] General
Maurice, and Viola Parsons, whom I hadn't seen for
a year. The Munnings had agreed to take Augustus
John's house in Chelsea, and were going into possession
now, when at the last moment John refused to sign
the agreement, and has since been lost in the wilds of
Spain. Viola has been on a long provincial tour, but
hopes for a London engagement in the early Autumn.
Irene has sent us a Box for *Belinda* to-night. I suppose you would still prefer *Loyalties* to anything else
for Wednesday.

[1] The Rt. Hon. C. F. G. Masterman and Mrs. Masterman.

I am afraid I am getting rather prolix. I have been making a speech at the morning sitting in the House about the Washington Treaty.

BEDFORD SQUARE,

20th July, 1922.

I hardly expected to get a letter to-day as I know you are taking your devious and tiresome journey. All the same I missed it. But I am looking forward to being with you on Saturday and Sunday. I wonder what you have been doing to-day, and whether you have succeeded in recalling the faithless Dominie [1] to his forsworn allegiance. I was sorry to hear this morning from Gilbert Murray that he and Lady Mary had been suddenly summoned to go to France to some place in the Auvergne, where Agnes, who was on her way back from one of her missions to Czecho-Slovakia, was lying critically ill. I do hope that this blow is not going to fall upon them.

The Russell divorce case, with its strange revelations as to the generation of babies, is the favourite topic of conversation in these last hours of the season. Sir J. Simon, who cross-examined " the Hart," seems

[1] John Sampson.

to have been heavily scored off by her. When he asked her (very foolishly) whether it wasn't "unusual" for a young married woman to use the bathroom of a bachelor, she replied at once : " Well, Sir John, isn't it better to be indiscreet than to be dirty ? "

I paid a short visit this morning to Anne,[1] who has a very well-formed baby about 16 days old. It is to be called Jane. Both are marvellously well.

Blessings,

H.

44 BEDFORD SQUARE, W.C.,

7th August, 1922.

I am sending you under another cover Sir F. Maurice's *Intrigues of the War*, which is well worth reading in a connected form.

To judge by what one reads in the papers, you must have had a tremendous downfall on Sunday. It rained pitilessly here all the afternoon, and rather spoilt the visit of a party of the younger students who came over from Oxford to have tea with us. There were about 30 of them, and they came in a char-à-bancs and motors. Beechman and his little company went

---

[1] Mrs. Cyril Asquith.

over to the Mill House and regaled us with one or two of the choruses from the Revue.[1] The words are not at all bad (tho' the singing was pretty indifferent), and they have devoted a good deal of attention to their make-up. They wrote to Clarkson to ask him if he had such a thing as an Asquith wig. He replied that he stocked them, and had three different ones for them to choose from. I suppose they have done duty in the pantomimes and some of the " Halls." The engaged pair—Isabella and Basil [2] —looked very happy ; they are like a couple of children, but tell me they are to be married in December.

Do you read Capablanca's vainglorious reports of his own play with the other " Masters " which he sends daily to *The Times* ? All the newspaper men in both hemispheres are completing and polishing up their obituary notices of Northcliffe, whose death is daily expected.

Keynes left us yesterday : he is good tho' freakish company.

I am just finishing the Life of Ballin, the great German shipowner. I think I shall find some useful material in it when I come to handle the Kaiser.

[1] The final event of the meeting of the Liberal Summer School at Oxford was the performance of a political revue.
[2] Isabella Rea and Basil Herbert.

Have you taken a turn yet at *The Second Empire* ? Guedalla and his wife were among our guests yesterday.

I am looking forward to coming on the 19th. I believe there is quite a good Golf Course at Lelant. The weather continues to be cold and depressing. I am delighted to hear that your house party get on so well.

I was looking just now in my Italian Grammar and came across one or two rather good proverbs, e.g. " *A chi la testa, non manca capello* " : " *La bella gabbia non nutre l'uccello* " : " *Pietra mossa non fa muschio.* " You should translate these. *Amerei essere sempre teco, e pure siamo sempre insieme ; non è vero ?*

THE WHARF,
SUTTON COURTENAY,

9th August, 1922.

The *Revue* last night was a marvellous success. There was no scenery and no orchestra, only a well-lighted stage and a piano, and a " beauty chorus " of well-dressed and for the most part nice-looking girls headed by Isabella Rea. The best acting was by Beechman, Basil Herbert, and Cope Morgan, all of whom (especially Basil) did their parts excellently, and sang distinctly and well. A trio (made up to resemble Donald Maclean, Simon and Runciman) with the " Three Little Liberals "—to the tune of " Three Little Maids from School "—was perhaps the success of the evening. Beechman impersonated me in one of the Asquith wigs, and amused the audience immensely. The libretto was of course light, but some parts of it, especially that given to Guedalla, were really witty. I think that Beechman is entitled to the lion's share of the credit. Donald Maclean and Phillipps went with us, and Simon was in the audience.

We are all going in to the final meeting, which is at 2 this afternoon, with E. Grey as principal performer, and our friend F. Gray [1] as second fiddle.

I had a long letter this morning from Rufus Isaacs who apologises for his silence, and gives quite an interesting account of Gandhi. Sir W. Tyrrell [2] has promised to help me in my Kaiser undertaking : he knows more of the pre-war history than anyone.

I must post this now. Tell me all about your doings.

THE WHARF,

13th August, 1922.

I am glad that you had a fine patch in which to make your expedition round the coast. Next time

[1] Frank Gray, then M.P. for Oxford.
[2] Lord Tyrrell, who was then Permanent Under-Secretary of State at the Foreign Office.

16

you should go the opposite way—North to Tintagel. The weather is unspeakable : I have only once been to play golf since I have been here. I am afraid you find the conditions (as you say) rather devitalising. I shall see you at the end of the week : would you rather I came Friday or Saturday ?

Three of the lines in the " Three Little Liberals " trio run in my head :

> Sir D.   I am a House of Commons star.
> Sir J.   And I am the leading light of the Bar.
> Mr. R.   And I'm for the bar where no drinks are.

Cope Morgan's Sir Donald was really very good : I do wish you had seen it.

Have you got a chess-board and men ?

I am irritated with the publishers for not sending me, as they promised, the advance proofs of the Kaiser's book. This is just the time I could have made real progress.

I see that Ll. G. is reported to be selling his memoirs for a fabulous sum.

John Buchan's latest " romance " *Huntingtower* is very well received. I think I will bring it with me when I come. There is a good account by Robert Lynd in *The New Statesman* of some obscure literary oddities of the 18th Century. One of them, Mary Collier, the poetical washer-woman of Petersfield, describes her retirement : " where I am endeavouring to pass the *relict* of my days in piety, purity, peace, and an old maid."

The greatest figure in the " simple school " was Ann Yearsley, " the Poetical Milkwoman of Bristol," who was compared by the blue-stocking Mrs. Montagu to Pindar and Æschylus.

I see Sir Albert Rollit is dead : he was for many years a figure in the House of Commons. He married in his old age the Dowager Duchess of Sutherland, the daughter of a head of a House, and one of the beauties of Oxford in my undergraduate days. She caught a Tartar, however, in tough old Rollit, who survived to be 82.

THE WHARF,
SUTTON COURTENAY,

15th August, 1922.

Northcliffe has at last come to his end, and the papers are full of him. The scribes have been at work for weeks on the topic—so congenial to them : for after all he was the Colossus of their world. So they have at last let loose a swollen torrent of the most nauseating " tosh."

Futility—the book about Russia—improves on fuller acquaintance, and, unlike most fiction that takes its rise in that soil and atmosphere, is at times extremely funny. Mr. Gerhardi, whoever he may be—and he writes quite good English—has a genuine sense of humour.

Margot's second book is at last finished and she is going to take the MS. up to Butterworth on Thursday. I can hardly guess whether it will be a success or not. I have just been looking over the chapter which deals with C.-B.'s death, and the early days of my Government : it has a number of good character sketches, especially that of John Morley.

Life is entirely without incident, and I look forward more than I can tell you to Friday.

Countless blessings.

THE WHARF,

28th August, 1922.

I hardly expected a letter this morning—such are the Sunday posts. But I hope I shall have one to-morrow.

I began work this morning in the Barn on the Kaiser, and read through his chapters on his two first Chancellors—Bismarck and Caprivi. It is not at all badly written, though rather *décousu* in style. He was

probably right to get rid of Bismarck—do you remember
Tenniel's famous cartoon " Dropping the Pilot " ?
—but he does not seem to have had any flair for
choosing men : partly because he suffered from the
first from the self-sufficiency (αὐθαδία) which grew on
him, and ultimately brought him to his doom. But
I think he will be an interesting study.

After I wrote to you yesterday I went to Boar's
Hill and saw Gilbert Murray, with whom I had an
interesting and at moments moving talk. Lady Mary,
whom I saw for a moment, is wonderfully brave,[1]
and is going at the end of the week with Gilbert to
Geneva, to the Assembly of the League of Nations.
It is almost stunning to think that Agnes should have
been cut down like this, when we see all these flimsy
girls leading their rotten and fruitless lives.

On my way back from The Mill, I looked in on
Mamma, who was gardening in her most vigorous
form. She seems to find *la vita sul Monticello molto
gaja*. The Keebles were coming to dine with her !
I reported well of you and the children at St. Ives.

Did you read the critiques of the new play *Bluebeard's Eighth Wife* ? We must go and see it : a
wonderful cast, Norman McKinnell, Madge Tithe-
ridge, etc., and (it seems) a really brilliant new actor

[1] Their daughter Agnes (see letter of 20th July) had recently
died.

named Hugh Wakefield. I was interested too in the account of a new musical setting to G. Murray's version of the *Alcestis* at Glastonbury. Steuart Wilson did the part of Admetus.

Margot has got a copy of *The Price She Paid*, of which I will tell you when I have read it.

All our guests have gone, except the family and poor old Paulto.[1] It is very peaceful, and I hope to do some work.

THE WHARF,

29th August, 1922.

We have really beautiful weather here : such as befits the beginning of autumn—for in three more days we shall be in September.

I spend my mornings in the Barn, reading and annotating the typescript of the Kaiser's book.[2] His pose, of course, is to shift all responsibility for the blunders and follies of his reign, both before and during the war, on to the shoulders of his Councillors and Ministers. He maintains that in all the serious crises he could never get his own way. I find him a really

[1] Harry Paulton.
[2] Mr. Asquith was at work on his own book *The Genesis of the War*. Cassell, 1923.

interesting study : not at all a simple personality, either for good or evil, or for wisdom or folly. He quotes rather a good German couplet :

" Unser König absolut,
Wenn er unser Willen tut " ;

which means in English :

"Absolute our King may be,
If he does what we decree."

I find it a real psychological puzzle, and I shall get Tyrrell, Drummond and others to supply me with detailed materials for a solution. I know, of course, the main lines.

Lucy [1] has just left on her return journey to Easton Grey. We chaffed her on her new Royal entanglements. I hope she will make, after all deductions, a net £300 on the transaction : but she will have to establish herself for the winter in a modest London flat.

Our friend Uccello is said to have woken up in the middle of the night and said suddenly to his wife— " Che bella cosa, il perspettivo ! " Quite a nice way of discovering a revolution in art. I long to hear from you.

All blessings.

[1] Mrs. Graham Smith, whose house was rented by the Prince of Wales for a few months.

THE WHARF,

31st August, 1922.

Thank you so much for your nice long letter. What a sad tale of misadventure ! I expect the Cornish trains—apart from the Riviera express—are no joke. I almost wept when I pictured you sitting in the dusky waiting-room with no better company than dead mackerel.

I am glad that you liked the characteristic climax of *Futility* : never was a book better named, but I have not for a long time read one that amused me so much. I am telling them to send you *Huntingtower* and *The Price She Paid*, which I began yesterday. I think the author is the same man who wrote *Susan Lennox*. It is quite clever, but so far the characters, one and all, are of unredeemed odiousness. One feels almost thankful that they could not have been created or have existed anywhere but in America, just as (in a different way) the Ibsens are Scandinavian and the Chekovs are Slavs.

Yesterday I went in the afternoon to Huntercombe and played eleven or twelve holes, when we were driven in by the rain. I was playing at least two strokes a hole better than on that ill-starred adventure of ours at Lelant. I was catching my drives and

sending the longish approach putts time after time
to within six inches of the hole ! I wished you had
been there—and the Grants : [1] we would certainly
have laid them low : even though Sir H. had tried the
" snatching " game, as he did when your ball found
a temporary grave in the churchyard. I was more
than irritated at the contrast.

l had a letter this morning from Princess Marie
Louise of Schleswig-Holstein, asking me to " write
something " on a very little blank book about two
inches square, to form part of the library of the
Queen's Dolls' House, in which (she says) " everything that one would find in a King's Palace to-day
is reproduced with minute accuracy : so that it will
have *great historical value* in the future." Orpen has
been commandeered to do a picture of the Queen in
her Coronation robes, for which she has offered him
a sitting.

Woodruff (who acted in the *Revue* and is President
this year of the University Liberal Club) has asked me
to dine with them at Oxford on Sat. Nov. 4th, and I
mean to do so. Meanwhile I hope a Scotch seat is
being found for our friend Sir Grant at Roxburgh and
Selkirk.

Vivian Phillipps has been spending a fortnight with
his family in Rhineland : they were a party of five,

---

[1] Sir Hamilton and Lady Grant.

and, with the mark at 7,000, they lived in the best hotels with bathroom, sitting-rooms, etc., at an average cost of 5s. a day each : " truly," as he says, " the family man's holiday paradise."

Do you know this story of Addison, who, though the most popular author of his day, was (like Goldsmith later) a wretched talker ? " Madam," he said to a lady, who had politely referred to the contrast, " I have only ninepence in ready money, but I can draw for a thousand pounds." On the other hand, there is Burnand's remark to George Meredith : " Damn it, George, why can't you write like you talk ? " I still think G. M. the best talker I have ever met.

I do my daily toll in the Kaiser business. So far I have only made notes and queries as I go along ; when I am well saturated I don't think I shall find the actual writing very difficult.

I am looking out of the Barn window, and see a knot of friendly tourists across the river snap-shotting the house. It reminds me of our friends at Gurnards Head.

Clifford Sharp is here for two or three days. Though he writes as well as ever, he is not so quick as he was in conversation. Ronald Lindsay of the Foreign Office, Elizabeth's friend, who came for the night yesterday, told me an amusing thing. In or about 1896 we were on the verge of war with the United States over a quite trumpery quarrel about Venezuela, in which we ultimately and very wisely climbed down. At the height of the dispute Lord Salisbury wrote a very tart and provocative despatch, which by mistake was put into the Foreign Office bag for *Pekin* instead of that for Washington. It was perhaps what is called a providential blunder, for it allowed time for the atmosphere to cool.

I must stop now, ἀγαπητοτάτη, and return to my Kaiser. A week ago to-day we were admiring together the masterpieces of " Gert Harvey." It seems an age.

THE WHARF,

1st September, 1922.

I had no letter this morning : I suspect our posts to you are much better than yours to me. We are suffering from a bad spell of foul weather. The result is that I have had a solid morning *à deux* with the Kaiser. I have now read the whole of his book except two or three chapters. He was a dabbler and a smatterer and a super-dilettante in almost every department : he particularly fancied himself, after he bought the Achilleion at Corfu, as an expert in all the developments of Greek sculpture and architecture. He was, of course, always coached and devilled by sycophantic German professors ; but it is only fair to admit that he had a wider range of interests than any royal person since Napoleon. I wish you were here that I might read aloud to you some of his amazing *écartades* : at any rate it is not at all dull.

I thank God that we have at last got to September, so that in less than a fortnight I shall see you again.

THE WHARF,

3rd September, 1922.

Thank you so much for your letter. Li T'ai Po was evidently a real poet : he flourished as far back as the Sung era, A.D. 700, when the whole of Europe could not produce a couplet of even third-rate verse. I hope you got the books from Bumpus. I became growingly irritated with *The Price She Paid,* and skipped quite a lot of it. The characters, whether good or bad, and they are for the most part repellent, are not the least like real people, and long before the end one ceases to have any interest in what is to become of Mildred. The worst of it is that the book begins quite well and the author has real descriptive power.

The Holdens came here on Friday for a couple of nights. What I like about them is their vitality and high spirits and good nature.

Colonel House, the American, who during the war was President Wilson's *âme damnée*, and has since (like all his friends) quarrelled with him, is coming from London to lunch to-day (Sunday) : he wants to talk to me about Reparations and Debts, etc., of " sackbuts and of psalteries, and whether shawms have strings." It is exceedingly difficult to keep an American to a single point at a time.

I have finished reading the Kaiser, and before I begin to write seriously, I find I must soak myself in the Memoirs of Tirpitz, Bethmann-Hollweg, Haldane and others : all of whom have written copiously on different aspects of the same theme.

You will have entered now upon what is practically the last week of St. Ives. I think it was a lucky choice. I wonder if you went to the weekly orgy at Newlyn last night, and what time you got back home. I suppose that by now the Grant family have *fait leurs paquets* and decamped to the North.

Violet and Bongie go to Scotland to-night for a month. We have no visitors in prospect here, except Sir W. Tyrrell and perhaps the Spenders for a night or two.

THE WHARF,

4th September, 1922.

Colonel House came to lunch yesterday and I had
two very interesting talks with him. He has thoroughly sound ideas about our debt to America : that
we ought to continue to express our wish and ability
to pay, but that America ought to seize the first oppor-
tune moment to refuse to go on receiving it. We can
only pay in gold—of which she has more than enough
—or in goods which would compete with hers in her
own market and which she has just finished building
up a huge protective tariff to exclude. Never was
there such an absurd situation. He told me a number
of curious things about President Wilson, who, but for
his perverse and tactless arrogance, could easily have
got the assent of the Senate both to the Treaty and to
America joining the League of Nations. He ascribed
both Wilson's and Roosevelt's paralytic strokes to the
same cause—violent hatred, in the one case of the
Senate, and in the other of Wilson himself, whom, he
says, he loathed with passion " morning, noon and
night." House himself is a curious study : he has
never been in Congress, or held any office, or (so far
as I know) ever spoken on politics in America : but
he was *Son Eminence Grise* (as the French used to say of

Richelieu's understudy) during all the best days of Wilson, who would have been saved from disaster if he had continued to take his advice. He went back to London soon after lunch.

I had a letter this morning from the Poet Laureate [1] in which he tells me that he had "strange influx of the Muses' juice, or whatever it be, last year," and as a result has a "good lot" of poems ready for printing, which he thinks "in some respects better than anything I have done before." If they resemble one that I saw in *The Times* the other day on some commemoration, I rather tremble. With the strange passion for scientific rhythm, and accent, and "homonyms," etc., etc., which has been growing on him of late years, I am afraid he will not have given the "juice" a fair chance.

Talking of commemorations, I thought that we had by now erected a monument to every conceivable benefactor. But I see to-day that the City of Strasbourg is about to put up a bronze statue in honour of the inventor of *pâté de foie gras*—one Close, who flourished about 1765. Who can set a limit to human folly?

I sent back the booklet for the Dolls' House Library, with a sentence from one of my own speeches!

[1] Dr. Robert Bridges.

In the intervals of Kaisering, I have been reading some of the critiques of *East of Suez*. Maggie Albanesi and an actress named Ault, whom I have never seen, seem to have scored heavily. But it reads like a rather thin story overloaded with local colour. All the same, I think we must go and see it.

It is quite a long time since I visited the Hill. I think I must go some afternoon and look up Jan.

I read some more Gibbon last night. I delight in him, but he takes time to masticate and digest. Tell me all about yourself and how you are going to spend these last days.

All blessings and love.

THE WHARF,

5th September, 1922.

I was sad not to hear from you this morning : Saturday to Tuesday is a long time in itself and tomorrow is Wednesday. I hope you got mine which was posted at Henley of all places.

Lord Kilbracken has just arrived for lunch. He is Hugh Godley's father and I suppose about 77,[1] but with few, if any, signs of age. He was the most dis-

[1] He was actually 75.

31

tinguished Balliol man of his time, and then after serving as Gladstone's private secretary he went to the India Office as permanent Under-Secretary, and was the real Governor of India under a succession of Viceroys and Secretaries of State for the best part of thirty years. He is a highly cultivated man, with a vast knowledge of literature, but with all the characteristic limitations of the Civil Servant type, amongst which is excessive caution and non-committalness. It used to be said of one of the most distinguished of them, Sir Alfred Lyall, who was a poet to boot, that even on such a topic as the weather he would not go further than : " I am inclined to guess that there is a touch of East in the wind : but of course you mustn't give me away."

Col. House told us an American story (which used to be applied to President Roosevelt) of a small boy saying to his mother : " Mother, I am the best boy in the school." " Who told you so ? " " I found it out for myself."

I am now studying the Kaiser, not as he sees himself (like the small boy), but as others see or saw him : Tirpitz, Bethmann, Ballin, etc. Do you see that he is going to marry a young widow of 35 ? It is another case of the widow wins.

Later. Lord K. has gone. He talked well, full of reminiscences of Gladstone, etc. I am sure the middle

Victorians were a hardy generation. He told us that seventy years ago he went round the world as a child of five or six, in two sailing-ships—to and from Australia and New Zealand. They rounded on one voyage the Cape of Good Hope and on the other Cape Horn. Each voyage took 103 days, and he says that coming round the Horn they never saw land for a hundred days, when they at last sighted the Lizard ! He asserts that in the Navy and Mercantile Marine of to-day he cannot find anyone who has been more than a fortnight out of sight of land. He is not in the least deaf or blind and has a marvellous memory. Another proof that age is not to be measured by the calendar.

THE WHARF,

7th September, 1922.

I hope your char-à-bancs adventure went off well. You must have been a huge and miscellaneous party. I trust that you had the right sort of weather. Here we are basking in a second summer : yesterday and to-day the sun has shone vaguely and there is no nip in the air.

W. Tyrrell came here for the night and was interesting about foreign matters. The Greeks are in a really bad plight, and though I am no Turk-lover

I cannot pity them, having chosen as they did Tino and the worse part.[1]

All our birds of passage have now migrated, and, as Elizabeth is in London to-day, we are reduced to Margot, Puffin and me, plus Harry Paulton, who does not come in to any meal : he leads the life of a complete invalid except for his nightly rubbers of bridge.

I am sending in the first instalment of my Kaiser to be typewritten by the people in the Broad. I have rather enjoyed doing my little sketch of Bismarck. And I have got in one or two knocks at the Kaiser over his foolish catch-word : " The encirclement of Germany."

I see that an Arnold Bennett play is about to be produced by Nigel Playfair with (among others) Viola Tree in the caste. Altogether the autumn theatre seems promising. I am glad to think that in another week you will be back on the Hill.

THE WHARF,

12th September, 1922.

I was delighted to get Anne's little present and your dear message. I have had countless telegrams,

[1] The Greek Army was completely defeated by the Turks in Asia Minor, and Greece had to request the Great Powers to negotiate an Armistice. On Sept. 9th, Turkish forces occupied Smyrna, and the evacuation of Anatolia by the Greeks was practically completed.

including a warm one from the King, but none that I cared for so much as yours. I have had some very attractive presents from the family and others. Elizabeth and Puffin are the only children here, and we have in addition the Derenburgs, the returned Hartley [1] (who is going to attempt a fresh start to Venice to-morrow) and Jack Macdougall. All we want for a placid commemoration is more sunshine.

I hope you will get through your cross-country journey to-morrow without hitch or undue fatigue. I shall come to see you on Thursday. I think you have had a very successful holiday.

I am now in daily contact with the typewriter company in the Broad. They sent me to-day a charming little *faux pas*. I quoted the Kaiser as saying of his second Chancellor Caprivi, that " he left his post in a calm and dignified manner." This appears in the transcript : " he left his post in a *cab*, and dignified manner." It was lucky my eagle eye detected the error.

44 BEDFORD SQUARE, W.C.1,

17th November, 1922.

Thank you so much for your letter this morning. I could not write yesterday as I was all day in the train.

[1] Leslie Hartley, novelist and critic.

I went to the counting at Paisley [1] shortly before midnight on Wednesday, and watched the process until about 1.30 a.m. when the result was declared. We had been assured that all was more than safe, so that I was not a little surprised to find when I arrived that it was beginning to look like a neck-and-neck affair. I had quite an exciting hour while the numbers fluctuated up and down, keeping on the whole almost even : indeed, it was not till the last quarter of an hour that we forged ahead, and proceeded to win (as the racing people say) " cleverly." I polled more votes than I did three years ago, and the drop in the majority was entirely due to the enormous addition to the Labour vote, owing to the 5,000 unemployed in Paisley (of whom there were none in 1920) and the sullen anti-bourgeois feeling which is swelling like a tidal wave over the whole of the West of Scotland. My people are not the least disconcerted : all they care for is to win ; and we had a marvellous farewell meeting at the Liberal Club between 2 and 3 a.m.

The general result does not greatly surprise me. The suicide of the Coalition before the election took much of the punch out of the fight, and left the country divided between Tranquillity and Socialism. It will be interesting to see how the thing develops.

[1] The General Election of Nov. 1922.

For the moment the thing that gives me the most satisfaction is to gloat over the corpses which have been left on the battlefield, Winston, Hamar Greenwood, Freddie Guest, Montagu, Kellaway—all of them renegades—and among the lesser fry Harry McLaren. I am terribly disappointed at the loss of Donald Maclean and Geoffrey Howard. They are both most difficult to replace.

Thank Anne for her delightful letters. I am pleased to know that she is so keen. Your man Lloyd seems to have had a pretty hard fight to keep his seat.

I have had H. Gladstone and Sir R. Hudson with me all this morning, and to-morrow I must see and talk over things with poor Donald Maclean. I very much fear I shall not be able to get to The Wharf in time to see you, but you may look for me without fail on Sunday morning.

Antoine arrived a day or two ago, and he and Eliz. are coming to lunch in a few minutes from now. They leave for America to-morrow week.

Countless blessings.

44 BEDFORD SQUARE,

21st November, 1922.

To-morrow I am going to the opening by the Prince of Wales of the memorial to the House of Commons'

fathers and sons who fell in the war, at the end of
Westminster Hall, and then to a lunch they are giving
at the National Liberal Club to poor Donald.

You have a Coleridge—haven't you ? Look at the
Ode to *Tranquillity* (which is not at all Bonar-Law-ian) :
the last four lines are as fine in their way as anything
can be. What a genius ! fuddled with opium,
obfuscated by bad German metaphysics, and finally
squandering itself like a fountain spraying into desert-
sand. There is no more tragic figure in literature.
A " Lone Arab " indeed. I had a search at The
Wharf on Sunday for the actual Arab lines : neither
I nor Desmond (who knows his Coleridge well) could
find them. The present generation do not know
their way about these trackless wilds, and to my
thinking have no *real* sense of perspectives or values.

I had a visit this morning from Mr. Flower—the
literary editor of Cassells, who came to talk about
my book. He evidently thinks it is going to be too
meticulous and elaborate. I gave him no encourage-
ment, and said I must do it my own way—or not at all.
In the end he acquiesced and went courteously away.
I suppose publishers have always been the same—
from the days of Jacob Tonson and Edward Cave
downwards. Dr. Johnson, who owed his livelihood
during his struggling years to Cave, thought that
Strahan (a Scotchman) was the best. Do you ever

turn over your Boswell now? You will find them all there, together with that priceless bookseller Mr. Dilly, at whose table Johnson met and was fascinated by John Wilkes.

Antoine and Elizabeth leave on Saturday by the *Aquitania*. We have a little farewell dinner for them on Friday night.

44 BEDFORD SQUARE,

28th November, 1922.

Thank you so much for your letter. My cough is less troublesome, but refuses to disappear.

Things here (not in the House itself, but in its purlieus) are interesting and not without their comic side. There was a kind of " fraternity " gathering last night in one of the Committee rooms between the rank and file of our lot and the ex-Coalie Liberals. The latter seem prepared to " re-unite " on almost any terms. Do you remember the marvellous chapter in Carlyle's *French Revolution* on the " baiser de Lamourette "? It looks as if it would soon come to that. I am all against forcing the pace and surrendering any of our ground. Meanwhile Ll. G. is evidently dallying with visions of reconciliation. He took Hogge [1] (of all

[1] J. M. Hogge, M.P., Whip to the Independent Liberals.

people) into his room last night and talked to him for an hour and a half in his most mellifluous vein. Amongst other things he declared that he was quite ready to serve with and under me (!), with whom he had never had a quarrel and whom he had never ceased to admire and respect ! There are among the new members of both sets a lot of greenhorns and *gobe-mouches*, and they are very much alarmed. Bonar has a very weak team, except the new Attorney-General, Douglas Hogg,[1] who seems to be a capable man and good debater.

44 BEDFORD SQUARE,

7th December, 1922.

I finished *Babbitt* last night and will bring it with me to-morrow. I don't expect you will like it : a squalid film of sordid American bourgeoisie in a petty environment and without any kind of " uplift." But one feels that it is absolutely true to life, with no fakes or illusions ; almost pitiless realism, but the work of a real artist.

Lord and Lady Lansdowne came to see us this morning : he is the last survivor, with the possible

---

[1] Now Lord Hailsham.

exception of Crewe, of the type of Grand Seigneur. The mould is broken and will never be re-cast. He has amongst other things a great knowledge of pictures, of which he has a fine collection at Bowood. Buckmaster came to lunch—full as always of life and spring, with a certain almost childish naïveté of simplicity and charm.

We have our weekly Party meeting in an hour's time : they have done very well in the two crucial divisions, and every one of them has been accounted for, and last night the Government's majority fell to 50. I shall drive down to-morrow after lunch and shall be with you for dinner at Sandlands.

I had a letter from young Marjoribanks [1] asking me to dine with him to-night before the Union, which of course I couldn't do.

All love and blessings.

44 BEDFORD SQUARE, W.C.1,

1st February, 1923.

I was more than delighted to get your letter and magnificent translation, which was all but word

[1] Edward Marjoribanks, afterwards the biographer of Sir E. Marshall Hall and Lord Carson.

perfect, some of the stiffest stiles having been neatly and deftly leaped. The only thing I wished was that it should have been complete. I liked Anne's agitation at the approach of " Carline "[1] ; like mother like daughter !

The wedding yesterday was quite a success, as such things go ; the P. of Wales and I signed the register. I have rarely seen a more attractive bride. I went for twenty minutes this morning to give a final sitting to Miss Franklin (daughter of one of our rich Jew London candidates, a niece of Sir H. Samuel), who has a studio near Paddington station, and hoped to exhibit my bust at the Academy ! It was in marble, and all her strokes were made with hammer and chisel. I went on to the Grosvenor Gallery, which is given up to Lavery and W. Rothenstein. I was disappointed with Rothenstein's red chalk heads. Of course he draws well, but has little sense of likeness. I found Lavery there ; he is a delightful fellow with no vanity. Amongst his themes is the one he did of the view from the garden (seven years ago) with the two punts in the foreground, containing Violet, poor old H. Paulton, Elizabeth and the dog. Far the best of his was a really good landscape (nearly twenty years old) of Barbizon bridge at Fontainebleau—very like the bridge at Abingdon. We have had a political lunch,

[1] Sydney Carline, late master of the Ruskin Drawing School.

and I shan't get to The Wharf much before dinner, so to see you to-night is impossible.

THE HOUSE OF COMMONS,

15th February, 1923.

I was delighted with your letter. Did you realise that yesterday combined the Fast of Ash Wednesday and the Feast of St. Valentine, a saint who seems to be quite out of fashion these latter days.

I sat all the morning listening to arguments in the arbitration between the British and Canadian Governments. It was like old times, and though the actual issue is juiceless enough, there were some nice points raised and I quite enjoyed it. Simon came to lunch : also Frances Horner,[1] who strongly recommended *Fiery Particles*—a book of short stories by C. E. Montague, who is, at his best, quite a good writer. I shall get it, as I have nothing at present for bedside reading except the Dictionary of National Biography.

I stumbled across old T. P. O'Connor in the Lobby last night : he is the senior M.P., what we call

[1] Lady Horner.

the " Father of the House," and in age somewhere
between 75 and 80. He is just starting a new magazine, and after saying some nice things about my
speech went on to extol the old stagers. He told me
he had got a new slogan, and when I asked what it
was he replied, " I'm damned if I'll be buried before
I'm dead." Don't you think it very good ? It
reminded me of what Antony says of himself in
Antony & Cleopatra : " There's sap in't yet."

Mr. Frank Gray of Oxford pervades the place and
constantly button-holes me and has a " few words."
One of the Labour men last night, exasperated by
Nancy Astor's perpetual interruptions, exclaimed :
" You have not the manners of a street-corner cat."
I am just going to a meeting of our little Party, who
are in good fettle, though I gather that outside there
is much perturbation among the faithful at our com-
bining in a joint amendment with the Coalies. They
think that we ought not to handle the unclean thing,
and I have a good deal of sneaking sympathy with
them. But we shall give the Coalies an awkward
quarter of an hour on Tuesday, when we force them
to divide on Mesopotamia.

I fear I shall not see you till Sunday morning, as
this arbitration will prevent me from leaving early
on Saturday.

All blessings.

44

House of Commons,

27th February, 1923.

Thank you for your letter. I agree that " music " —in our sense—would make a very good subject for you. In the intervals of wielding the brush you will do well once more to handle your pen.

After a steady day's work I left The Wharf at about 5 yesterday afternoon. The hound took his place beside me in the car, and on our arrival at Bedford Square resumed his seat on my mantelpiece, where he now gazes once more, after weeks of separation, upon his fellow : one is almost inclined to fancy that they both relish their re-union.

Someone left behind at The Wharf a book by an American playwright, of whom I have never heard before, one Eugene O'Neill—evidently of Irish extraction. I began to read it in the car driving up— without any expectations—and was much interested. There are only three plays in it—all of them belonging to *le genre sombre*, but not in the least foul or even coarse. I shall be very curious to see what you think of it, and will bring it back with me for you on Saturday. They are quite unlike anything that we read in these days, and I am not sure how they would act on the stage. The Americans are already far ahead of us in fiction : Harrison, Edith Wharton, Sinclair Lewis : but hitherto they have not produced in these days a good dramatist. Margot went yesterday afternoon to a matinée of the terrible exposure of Welsh life *Capel Sion* (I mean the book) which has just been dramatised by the author, who bears the name of " Caradoc Evans." She reports that it reminds one of the corresponding picture of the squalors and freaks of the Irish Arcadia, *The Playboy of the Western World*, which, however, contains one of the best love-scenes, if not the best, in the 19th-century drama.

I am so glad that you are pleased with T. B. Old John Lane the publisher came to lunch to-day : Lucy also. He is an odd fish who knows a lot about out-of-the-way culs-de-sac in both literature and art. Margot and Lucy set off after lunch to an afternoon meeting in Willesden on behalf of Crinks Johnstone, at which Violet was to be the principal speaker. She starts on her fortnight's visit to stay with the D'Abs. at Berlin to-morrow night.

I am going to dine to-night, as I do once or perhaps twice a year, at " The Club "—Dr. Johnson's—but alas ! there are no Burkes or Garricks, or even Boswells, to be found there now.

44 Bedford Square, W.C.1,

7th March, 1923.

I loved your letter. At last I heard from Dobbie this morning. I see that you are going to take them to lunch on Saturday with an American poet unknown to me. I hope to see you later in the day.

We must go and see *The Bad Man* together ; it is just our sort of play. I gather from the critiques to-day that Milne has produced a mediocre affair, which is a pity.

We dined last night at the Palace, and, as I murmured to my neighbour, marvelled upon the problem of upon what principle of selection they assort their guests, e.g. Lord Lonsdale and Rudyard Kipling. I had quite a good talk with the former about hunting, coursing, boxing and other congenial topics. The King was in his usual form and very friendly : I reminded him how, on the night of the 1st of August 1914, I invaded the Palace with W. Tyrrell at 1.30 a.m., and he appeared with sleepy eyes in his pyjamas and dressing-gown, and signed a telegram which we had drawn up to " Nikky " of Russia. I also had a talk with the Queen (who said that Mary II was doing wonderfully) mainly about her dolls' house, which is now at the " Kid's " [1] in Appletree Yard and won't be finished for another year ! She means to find it a *gîte* at Windsor.

I am just off to Cambridge, and the typist is hurrying to put my speech into form for the London press. I shall be back early to-morrow, so write.

44 BEDFORD SQUARE, W.C.1,

8th March, 1923.

Thank you so much for your letter which I found on my return from Cambridge this morning. If it is fine, we might golf together at Huntercombe on Saturday afternoon. I would bring you to lunch. It is a dreary looking sky to-day, but the sun may return before then.

Don't be depressed about your drawing : sooner or later the spark will quicken and " suffuse the whole clod."

I hope you approved of my speech at Cambridge : it seems to have given a good deal of satisfaction here. It was a very jolly meeting : 150 undergraduates with

[1] William Nicholson the artist.

a sprinkling of dons at dinner made a very enthusiastic audience. I don't think the young men speak quite as well as those at Oxford, but they are a very forthcoming and attractive type. A particularly nice young Haldane [1] —nephew of our illustrious friend— was in the chair. I sat next to a young Fellow of Clare—Henderson by name—said to be a brilliant economist : he has just been appointed, in succession to Massingham, editor of *The Nation*, in which Keynes and his group have acquired a controlling influence. There was a really amusing attempt at a " rag." Just after my train had started at 5 yesterday, a telegram was received by our young friends at Cambridge, dispatched from Notting Hill Gate, and purporting to come from me, to the effect that I was indisposed and could not come to dinner. They were of course in despair, but fortunately they resolved to run no risks and came to the station and met me when I arrived. The hoaxers were also there—some seven or eight stalwart undergraduates—whose plan was to meet me under the pretence that they were my hosts (of course I shouldn't have known the difference) and then to escort me in their motor, which would have rapidly whisked me off to Royston (about ten or twelve miles away), where I should have been kept in durance for two or three hours and only brought back to Cambridge after the dinner was over. It was rather a

---

[1] J. B. S. Haldane.

novel idea, borrowed, I suppose, from what is going on in Ireland. My bodyguard, who appeared in full force at the station this morning, are determined to track down the would-be raggers and give them " snuff."

We have just had a very enthusiastic meeting of our little party in the House.

The Jowitt [1] baby is going to be christened in the House of Commons crypt to-morrow at 3, and I am bidden to the ceremony. I have to dine in the evening at the Speaker's State Dinner, from which one cannot escape.

Blessings.

HOUSE OF COMMONS,

24th April, 1923.

Thank you so much for your letter. " Gala Week " [2] develops with rapidity and rigour : tiers of seats and fleets of masts are rising all round Westminster. I went in my knee-breeches and medals after dinner to

---

[1] Sir William Jowitt.

[2] The preparations for the marriage of the Duke and Duchess of York.

Buckingham Palace, where the rooms, big as they are, were very nearly crowded. There were huge glass cases like you see in the Bond St. shops, filled with jewels and every kind of gilt and silver ware. The bride, everyone says, is full of charm and stood in a row with the King and Queen. We all shook hands with her as we passed. Mingling in the crowd I came across Princess Mary, who was in quite good looks, and we interchanged a few pleasantries. The whole of what is called the " world " was there in its best frocks. I had a talk, among others, with Lord Leverhulme (of Sunlight Soap), who is nearly as deaf as a post but a remarkable man in his way. He was an assistant behind the counter in a small grocer's shop in Lancashire 40 years ago, and now owns and controls the largest business in Europe. He is also a great collector of pictures and Oriental china. I got away pretty early : the pictures in the big rooms and corridors of Buckingham Palace are always a delight to see.

This morning, after seeing some men on business, I went before lunch for half an hour to the Mansard Galleries to see the productions of the London group, including Dobbie's bust of Anne. It is a very graceful and attractive bit of work. The show as a whole I thought very indifferent. Both Sydney and Richard Carline are among the contributors, and I thought Sydney's little group of women bathers one of the most satisfactory things there : not at all ambitious, but what the critics call " pleasing," and both well drawn and well coloured. Seabrooke I thought distinctly disappointing, and neither of the Nash's is good. I enclose the catalogue.

I went to Victoria at 5 this afternoon to meet Margot, who was in excellent condition and is going to-night with Puffin to see the gloomy " Christie " [1] play. I am dining with the Australians. I hope you haven't forgotten to send me your address at Sandown. I assume from your silence that Anne is all right again. It is sad that I shan't see you till the end of the week.

Blessings.

44 BEDFORD SQUARE, W.C.1,

26th April, 1923.

I was much delighted to get your letter. The crowds in the streets were enormous, and though during the actual wedding it was fine I am afraid a lot of them must during the day have been drenched

[1] *Anna Christie*, by Eugene O'Neill.

to the skin. I won't bore you with an account of
the ceremony, which resembled very much that of
Princess Mary a year ago. As a pageant it was
extremely well done. I sat in the stalls with a curious
little knot of neighbours : Ramsay MacDonald and
Clynes (who were in black frock-coats), Buckmaster,
Simon and Winston Churchill ! The ennui of the
long waits was relieved for me by being next to
Winston, who was in his best form and really amusing.
Between two fugues (or whatever they are called) on
the organ, he expounded to me his housing policy :
" Build the house round the wife and mother : let
her always have water on the boil : make her the
central factor, the dominating condition, of the
situation," etc., etc.—in his most rhetorical vein.
Out of the proceeds of his book he has bought a
modest country house and 80 acres of land in Kent,
and is busy rebuilding and developing. I suggested
that he should call it (after the title of his book) " The
World Crisis." He has sold 10,000 copies of his first
volume at 30s. and hopes to reap a second harvest
by a cheap edition at 10s.

I am going to-night with Puffin and one of his
friends to see the Marionettes and will report to you.
P. goes back to Oxford for the new term to-morrow.
I have been reading about prehistoric man in the
new Cambridge history. I am speaking at Bourne-

mouth next Friday, May 4th—in reply to Ll. G. who speaks at Manchester this Saturday.

44 BEDFORD SQUARE, W.C.1,

27th April, 1923.

We had our weekly Party meeting at the House last night, and I found them all in good fettle. We are awaiting Ll. G.'s latest gyrations at Manchester to-morrow.

I went after dinner with Puffin to the Marionettes. From the mechanical point of view, they are marvellously conceived and manipulated inventions and were worth seeing. During the first hour they did a series of disconnected " stunts " which were very entertaining. Then alas ! they plunged into a full-grown modern Italian Opera, in three acts—full of trills and caratinas, and all the familiar tricks of that most arid form of composition : the singing being supplied by unseen and full-throated " humans " behind, while the poor marionettes strutted and gesticulated in dumb show in front. There were some quite good moments, but one was impressed, and in time rather wearied, by the incongruity and unnaturalness of the whole thing. I can see that it won't have a long run.

Viola [1] came to lunch to-day (with Clifford Sharp and Spender and other grave people). She is making quite a small fortune out of her " Dancers," and she could well afford to be tolerant of my good-humoured gibes. They have sold the American rights for a good sum. On the other hand, *The Gay Lord Quex*, in which she has a part, is rapidly approaching its latter end. All the Pinero plays are now too datedly Victorian, and have had their day.

I looked in before lunch at the British Museum, to see their exhibition in the King's Library of the Folios and other Shakespearian relics. It is extremely interesting, and we must see it together. Amongst other curiosities, one sees how in less than twenty years the spelling of words changed : " historie," " comedie," " crueltie," etc., all coming to end with a *y*. This happened in Shakespeare's lifetime.

Puffin has just gone back to Oxford for the new term. We go to The Wharf to-morrow (Sat.) morning.

Did you see that one of the difficulties in the way of Summer Time in France is that farmers' wives object to getting up an hour earlier in the morning " to supply milk to the ladies of easy morals " in Paris and

[1] Viola Tree.

other big cities ? They are curiously in the dark as to the hours and ways of life of the demi-monde.

Hugh Cecil has sent me as a present copies of the proposed revision of the Prayer Book and the Psalter. I have been glancing through them with a certain amount of grim amusement. The bowdlerised Decalogue is really funny. These people live and move in a world which has no real existence.

I wonder what you are reading ? Dostoievsky ? or what ? Do tell me. Margot had brought me from Spain a wonderful Russian Ikon which I am going to install here among my books. Write.

44 BEDFORD SQUARE, W.C.1,

8th May, 1923.

Thank you so much for your note. I am glad you met G. B. S. He can be both agreeable and very amusing.

I had my first turn this morning with my new Private Secretary, Basil Herbert, whom you remember at Oxford and who married Isabella Rea. He is a very nice fellow, and seems alert and capable.

The Women's Liberal Federation is up for its annual session of two days, and Violet, who is their new President, delivered her inaugural address this morning. Margot was there and says it was very good—though I should think rather on the long side— nearly an hour. But hardly any of the women can speak really well, which she does. We are going to a ceremonial dinner given by Sir John and Lady Simon, to be followed by a huge reception of the faithful ladies, who have trooped up from all parts of the Kingdom.

We had quite a curious luncheon : Gladys Cooper, Philpot the artist, Charles Russell, Cynthia [1] and Lady Cunard. Gladys said that *Magda* [2] would carry her on till the end of the season : she goes every night at the close of the play an hour's drive in her motor to her country home, somewhere in Bucks. I have since been to a meeting at the Bank of England to discuss the payment of our American debt. I rather enjoyed it, as I met in the Governor's parlour five or six of the greatest financiers in the city. They were most welcoming, and it reminded me of the days when I was Chancellor of the Exchequer, an office I really liked. Write to me fully about your plans, and don't forget Dulwich.

Blessings untold.

[1] Lady Cynthia Asquith. [2] Sudermann's play.

44 BEDFORD SQUARE,

14*th May,* 1923.

I was amazed at the progress you have made in your drawing. It shows how foolish and inept it would be to start as the young men do on ambitious composition, without being thoroughly grounded in what underlies the whole thing. I hope there are no traces of the spread of the diphtheria epidemic on the Hill. You should be very careful about drinking water : better, I think, to have a few bottles of Malvern, and of course all milk ought to be boiled and sterilised. I expect the Dobbies were very happy and care-free with you.

Gilbert Murray brought his " big brother " to lunch at The Wharf. I liked him very much. He is enormously tall and spare and has a sun-dried complexion and skin of a man who has lived long in the tropics. He has been now for twenty years governing Papua—a sort of outlying spur of New Guinea, and, I should judge from his account of it, a most God-forsaken spot. It is fourteen years since he was last in England. You should read Pringle's excellent letter in *The Times* to-day.

I have two odd jobs of a peculiar kind on hand :
one (as I told you) to deliver this evening a short
allocution to the American Golf team ; and the other
to propose at a big House of Commons luncheon to-
morrow the health of " T. P." I finished last night
Beasts, Men and Gods, which you must read. It is
far more thrilling than *The Orissers.* I must give you
some sittings next week.

Blessings.

44 BEDFORD SQUARE,

16th May, 1923.

After I wrote yesterday I went into the House and
made a short speech about Russia, agreeing with
Ll. George !—which sounds suspicious. The Government practically climbed down, as they agreed to
negotiate here in London with Krassin.

I went to a little conclave at Abingdon St. this
morning to discuss the line which we should take
at the meetings a fortnight hence of the National
Federation. Edward Grey and a few of the inner
circle were there, and we found ourselves in harmony.
After lunch I paid another visit to the Bank of England
and discussed rather abstruse questions of finance

with the Governors and Lord Inchcape and other city pundits.

The new Editor of *The Nation* came to lunch to-day: he is a Cambridge economist, Henderson, and seems to be clever and alert.

The House adjourns for Whitsuntide to-morrow, and I shall come to The Wharf Friday and hope to go with you to Stratford on Saturday. Have you yet started on S. Antonio and the Fishes?

HOUSE OF COMMONS,

28th May, 1923.

I was sad yesterday when you disappeared down your little lane and were lost to sight. During the whole holiday week we never had a game of golf! On the other side of account, the drawing certainly made wonderful progress, and is very near to not only good but satisfying. One more effort, and I feel that you will have grappled with and triumphed over the most intractable of models.

I found out that Lady Bradford, who was one of our guests at this week-end, and who is as deaf as a post, is the mother of the child-genius, of whom we used to read in the days of *The Young Visiters*. She was then, at the age of 8 or thereabouts, a poetess, and now, when I suppose she is about 14, she has taken to drawing and painting, and is said to show such promise that her teachers can tell her little or nothing. She is a cousin of sorts to the Home Secretary Bridgeman, who has just been making a broken-backed, draggle-tailed defence in the House of his deportations and internments.

We had a short series of *éloges* of Bonar Law, which I thought very *mal à propos*, as the poor man is not yet in his grave. The new Prime Minister made a modest and unchallenging début.

I am reading over again at night Horace Walpole's *Castle of Otranto*—the real parent and forerunner of the whole tribe of Shockers.

All love.

HOUSE OF COMMONS,

29th May, 1923.

I went back to the House after dinner last night to vote, and was rewarded by hearing a really brilliant speech from Tom Mosley, who is one of our best recruits, and the more welcome to us, and hated by the Tories, because he is Lord Curzon's son-in-law.

I had an hour to spare before lunch to-day, and spent it more or less profitably in a solitary visit to two small picture exhibitions. The first was confined to the " works of Benjamin and Winifred Nicholson " at a small gallery at the end of Bond St. I met Lady Cecilia [1] coming out as I went in, and she gave me a word of warning. There are about fifty specimens— half the husband's and half the wife's—mostly oils, but with some dozen water-colours of hers. I came to the conclusion that she was by a long way the better artist of the two. Poor Ben is struggling to find a future which will reconcile his past and present. He is emerging from Vorticism. She is quite a good painter of flowers, and one of her water-colour land-scapes is really attractive. The gallery man told me that William Nicholson had looked in last night, and when asked his opinion of the show replied tersely and gruffly, " I did not come here as a critic."

I went on to the private view of Max's [2] things at the Leicester Galleries. Some of them are fiendishly clever, others I thought crude and exaggerated. In almost all of them the letter-press is better than the actual drawing. I met there, among other people, Gerald du Maurier and his wife and Lady Tree and

---

[1] Lady Cecilia Roberts.   [2] Max Beerbohm.

Maurice Baring. It is quite worth seeing, but the entrance charge to-morrow and afterwards, when it opens to the public, is ten shillings !

There is the great annual Flower Show at Chelsea to-day, and Margot, who went there, brought back our friend Miss Willmot—who is one of the judges— to lunch. She asked me whether I had re-visited the Shakespeare garden at Stratford. She is very anti-Bridges Adams. I had a very good talk on things in general at lunch with Clifford Sharp, who is, I think, now easily our best journalist.

The poor puppets have been put to an uncongenial task in an abridged version of *The Tempest*, and I gather that it did not quite come off. They ought to be kept to an Italian milieu.

To-morrow (Wed.) I am going to try to concoct something to say at Buxton on Friday. Tell me how you are faring with your new model.

All blessings, etc.

44 BEDFORD SQUARE,

5th June, 1923.

Thank you for your letter. We will have another sitting for St. Anthony : by the way, the Church has two St. A.s, separated by 1000 years : the one in the 3rd century, who was the founder of that foul institution *Monkery* : the other ours of Padua in the 13th. The Pig belongs to ours. But whether it was a pet, or a symbol (like the fishes) of what was worst in the lower nature of man seems to be a matter of dispute. I thought the composition of your schools of fishes quite excellent.

I looked in at the New English Arts Club's exhibition this morning, where there was an ambitious picture of St. Francis, with birds, etc., flocking around him, which was not nearly so good as yours. It is on the whole a poor show, and one of the best things in it is a portrait-study called " Peggy," by Sydney Carline : but, though well drawn and painted, I can't pretend that it is interesting.

What a marvellous vision for you to have had in the Cornmarket of those two tub-like figures interlinked !

The Aga Khan has just been here to lunch : he is going to take Margot to the Derby to-morrow, and pressed me to go with him to Epsom on Friday for the Oaks, in which he has a filly who is quite likely to win. As I shall only have just arrived after a night in the train from Paisley, I declined.

I am going to preside this afternoon at a dialectical duel between A. G. Gardiner and Philip Guedalla on Biography : it might be amusing.

I go to-night to Col. Faber's Derby dinner. I wish I could find a way to make a little money.

I was glancing this morning at a little life of Gainsborough which I have on these shelves. He and Sir Joshua were very jealous of one another, and from time to time G. refused to exhibit at the R.A. But each had a genuine admiration for the work of the other, and there is a story of G. going to the private view, and after surveying Sir Joshua's exhibits, exclaiming in a petulant voice : " Damn him : how various he is ! " A pretty compliment. They had a fine reconciliation at Gainsborough's deathbed, when he whispered to Sir J. : " We are all going to heaven, and Van Dyck is of the company."

I am going off to the House now to our little Party meeting, before I start for the duel. I wish you what Goldsmith called " eternal sunshine."

44 BEDFORD SQUARE,

2nd July, 1923.

We had a delicious time together. Your party was a raging success. I think dear Stennie [1] enjoyed him-

---

[1] Ernest Stenhouse, a neighbour on Boar's Hill.

self last night, and his last no-trumper enabled him to retire in a cloud of glory.

We had to lunch to-day Count Metternich who was German Ambassador here for a good many years—until two years before the war. He is a tragic figure : everything he had he invested here under Sir E. Cassel's advice, and the utmost that so far he has been able to recover from the wreckage is £200. When I asked him after lunch whether I should call a taxi, he replied No—that he always went now by bus. We had a very interesting talk about pre-war days, and the various ways in which the war might have been avoided or ended. I felt more than sorry for his sad fate.

There is nothing of any interest at the House, and I shall spend a solitary evening, as Margot and Puffin are going to the Vanderbilt Ball, where I have no desire to accompany them.

All my blessings.

44 BEDFORD SQUARE,

3rd July, 1923.

You shall certainly have the little white stag for a model. It will be a test of drawing : his lines are so clean and uncompromising.

My family are such inveterate pleasure hunters that I spent the evening here yesterday quite alone. I didn't mind much, as I had plenty to read.

After assimilating a little stuff for a short speech in the House this evening on Land Valuation, I went for an hour before lunch, first to Christie's, and then to Agnew's. Christie's are selling on Friday Robinson's —the South African millionaire's—large and expensively acquired collection of pictures. It is quite a remarkable show of almost all schools. There are some enormous Bouchers and others of the French genre of that age, which move me not at all. The two things that interested me were a pair of pictures by Piero di Cosimo (about 1490) of the adventures of Jason and Medea, and a pair of Ghirlandaios of St. John the Baptist and his mission. They reminded me of the best Florentines in the Ashmolean, and the freshness of the colouring is really gorgeous. I wish you could have been there, but they will all be dispersed on Friday. There was a mass of other good things, culminating in Gainsborough's fascinating " Mrs. Drummond." The more I see of him—and he is in competition here with Sir Joshua, Hoppner, Romney and Opie—the more I feel that he had something which none of them possessed or even shared. I went on to Agnew's, where there were only twenty pictures : I enclose the catalogue. You must come and see them. Far the cleverest and most original is Manet's " Le bon Bock." There are three Cézannes, but I feel more than ever sceptical as to his claims to be the " Second Adam " of Art. I would far rather have Degas at his best : as in " Le Foyer de la Danse." The tragedy is that there is nothing which we produce now which is in the *same class* with any of these.

I am just off to the House, and later to the unveiling of the Page Memorial by Edward Grey in Westminster Abbey.

Margot and Puffin went to the Vanderbilt Ball : the last word in American luxury. They are off this afternoon to the last stage but one of the Lawn Tennis at Wimbledon.

I pine for *Halicarnassus* ! [1]

Write to me.

HOUSE OF COMMONS,

16th July, 1923.

After I dropped you at Boar's Hill I had a strenuous afternoon piloting Mrs. Longworth [2] about the Oxford

---

[1] An imagined haven of peace and quiet.
[2] Daughter of the late Theodore Roosevelt.

Colleges. She is a strenuous sight-seer like her father, and (so ubiquitous are the American race) she came across an aunt and several cousins in the middle of New College chapel. She is a very intelligent woman and I like her.

I am afraid that Thursday would be a bad day to come to London. I have to be at the House for the Singapore debate, and our two bedrooms seem to be already bespoken. I doubt, too, whether *Melloney*[1] is worth the grind—even if it survives so long. I wish we could do something nice here before the shutters go up at the end of the month.

To-morrow morning I am going to see the King and Queen " re-open the roof " of Westminster Hall. It has been under reconstruction for quite ten years.

It is still hot, though now quite bearable.

I hope you will make progress with the stag to-morrow.

[1] *Melloney Holtspur*, a play by John Masefield.

THE LODGE,
KING'S COLLEGE,
CAMBRIDGE,

8th August, 1923.

Being here brings back our visit ever so long ago when we saw the *Oresteia* together. I wish you were here now. You would have enjoyed the *Cyclops* enormously : a marvellously good translation by Sheppard [1] (much better than the original), full of fun, and at times quite up to Gilbert and Sullivan. The performance was in the open air in the Fellows' Garden here, and the satyrs with their tails, the sheep and rams, Odysseus and the Cyclops himself were all acted with the greatest spirit and verve. The costumes were designed and painted by Duncan Grant, who is staying here. I met him last night, and I found him very agreeable. The singing of the Choruses was quite good. I will bring you the libretto.

Keynes gave us a little party in his rooms last night, and this morning I went to one of the lectures in the Summer School on " Trade Cycles," by Robertson (who played Silenus yesterday). He is a youngish

[1] The new Provost of King's.

don from Trinity, and an economist of great repute here. It was on the whole exceeding good, and he came well out of the heckling afterwards. Violet lunched with Cope Morgan—the Liberal candidate —at Trinity.

This evening we go to a lecture by Keynes on Currency, and after it there is the Revue—*Between Time and Tweed*—which ought to be amusing. There are to be thirty performers, male and female, all taken from among the Summer School Students. To-morrow (Thursday) I give the valedictory Address at 2, and we drive back to The Wharf in time for dinner.

I have been with you in spirit at Stratford to-day : I hope it went off well—despite the heat, which is tremendous here.

THE WHARF,

2nd September, 1923.

I can't tell you how much I miss my morning visits and talks. Writing is after all a poor substitute. I am hoping to hear to-morrow your first impressions of the Cove and its surroundings.

Cys and Anne are staying here now : also Ava Ribblesdale, who gave me a depressing account of her daily life. I feel less and less envy for the very rich.

I am now getting to work on the new book, and have dug out one or two very ancient *Spectator* articles, dating from 1876 and 1877, which I think may be pressed into the service : one on the Art of Tacitus, and another on the Age of Demosthenes. I will send you a copy of the *Genesis* as soon as I get one : some day, I suppose, this week.

It cleared up yesterday for our expedition to Whatcombe, where we again looked over Dawson's wonderful stables, and paid a long visit to Mumtaz Mahal, the marvel of the world. She is a great slashing creature, dark grey, and of perfect make and shape. No one knows how good she is, but I gather from Dawson that the Aga has been offered a fabulous sum for her : somewhere, I imagine, between £50,000 and £100,000. She cost £10,000 as a yearling, and is now 2.

I am well on now in the arrangement of the new book, and I don't know that there will be room for the new chapters. Among other things I am including " Reading and Writing," the " Last Crusade " and the " Antigone "—a rather varied menu.

The Japanese horror [1] exceeds anything of the kind that we know of in history. And it looks as if Mussolini has his eye on the permanent occupation of Corfu [2] : he has apparently just found out that it once belonged to Venice ! He appears to be, in the fullest sense, what Bethmann-Hollweg once called me, " a practical politician."

THE WHARF,

7th September, 1923.

I was glad to get your letter—the children seem to absorb a large share of your time and energies, while the Spark smoulders.

[1] The Earthquake of 1923.

[2] On 27th August three Italian members of the Græco-Albanian Boundary Commission were murdered in Greek territory. On the 29th Signor Mussolini demanded immediate satisfaction from Greece, and the next day occupied Corfu to enforce it. The day after Lord Oxford wrote the above letter, Greece brought up the question before the League of Nations and a serious difficulty was created by the Italian Government denying the competency of the League to deal with the question. A settlement was eventually reached through a Conference of Ambassadors, in which Italy agreed to evacuate Corfu, and Greece agreed to pay on 30th September 50,000,000 lire damages.

My book [1] was published yesterday and I am sending you yours. It is well turned out, but the price is too high. I saw a little pile on Blackwell's counter. The reviews, so far as I have seen any, are not unfriendly, tho' they are evidently disappointed that I have been so sparing of tittle-tattle.

The weather here has been divine, and Huntercombe was at its best. I hope it is treating you well. There is an almost lyrical effusion in *The Times* to-day from the parson of East Lulworth, who seems to be a rather light-headed person.

I was looking over old Crabb Robinson's Diary at the Mill House and came upon a neat retort. The famous Metternich congratulated Lord Dudley—who was for a short time Foreign Secretary—on the excellence of his French, adding that the common people in Vienna talked better French than educated Englishmen. " Your Excellency must remember," said Dudley, " that Bonaparte has not been twice in London to teach them."

I have been dipping into the new volume of Farringdon's Diary : very dull. I console myself with a few pages of my favourite P. G. Wodehouse.

[1] *The Genesis of the War*, Cassell.

THE WHARF,

10th September, 1923.

We are still most lucky in our weather, and it looks as if the good spell would last over my birthday. Mikky,[1] who spent Sunday here, left behind him a nice little present—a copy of the 1st edition of Fielding's *Voyage to Lisbon*, published (after his death) in 1755. He went out a dying man and is buried at Lisbon. He was only 48, born two years before Dr. Johnson.

I had some good talks with Hugh Cecil, who has a finer mind and much greater gifts of expression than Brother Bob. He is also a far better speaker—indeed, at his best not far from the best. It is a pity he should have lost his way in life in the labyrinths and quagmires of clericalism—not that he would ever have been a successful statesman in these days : he has too deep and unconcealed a loathing for democracy and what is called the Spirit of the Age. All which helps to make him an excellent companion.

There seems to be no getting to the end of Mussolini. One of the latest projects attributed to him—being ostensibly at any rate a devoted son of the Church—

[1] Sir Roderick Meiklejohn.

is to make it compulsory on all Italian workmen and peasants to have a crucifix in their homes. He seems to be getting all he wanted from the Greeks, and it is doubtful when, if at all, he will let go Corfu.

Do you remember this?

Lord Mansfield (of Stevens, the Shakespearian critic) : " We can only believe half of what Stevens says."

Dr. J. : " No one can tell *which* half."

THE WHARF,

11th September, 1923.

I am so delighted that you find the book to your taste. Though it does not appear on the surface, I often thought of you " between the lines."

I hope you had a good expedition to Poole. It was hardly a journey to test " Bluey's "[1] powers : I suppose, as the racing people say of the Aga's filly Mumtaz Mahal, she never had to " extend herself." Did you hunt up the illustrious Henry Lamb? I find, by the way, that Tonks was an ex-doctor. And

[1] His correspondent's motor-car.

76

were your eyes gladdened (and your heart lifted) by the fleeting vision of a Spencer ? [1]

I am glad that you have got your share of this wonderful summer weather.

I cannot pretend to be much affected by the thought that to-morrow is my birthday, though I suppose one ought to be compiling a rueful catalogue of wasted opportunities.   On the whole I am inclined to adhere to my old view—that the Quest is more than the Quarry. Do you remember what someone said of old Queen Charlotte—George III's wife—as she advanced in age ? " The bloom of her ugliness is going off."

How I wish you were within range, but I shall think of our favourite sonnet.

44 Bedford Square,

10th October, 1923.

We had a family dinner last night, from which Elizabeth was a bed-ridden absentee—Katherine, the Bebs, Betty, Nan, etc., with Gates and Ronald Lindsay. It went off very well.

[1] One of the two brother painters.

77

I am glad that you are going on with the "Widows." It is not altogether an easy composition. I looked in this morning at Burlington House to see the English Primitives. All told, they barely fill a couple of rooms. There is an excellent catalogue, full of learning, most of it spent in discussions whether this or that picture is really English in origin, and not German or Flemish. They are all supposed to date from 1300 to 1500. I can't say that any of them are remarkable either for beauty or technique, but they are quite worth seeing as a whole.

The Spanish Duke and Duchess of Alba, who were very kind to Margot in Spain, came to lunch : also Edwin Montagu, who has not been at our table for at least four years. He is going to India via South Africa and will be joined at Bombay in December by Cardy and Venetia. He is, as he always was, excellent company. He declares that the new Rothermere-Beaverbrook "combine" will mop up 75 per cent. of the newspapers of the country, with 5 million morning and 3 million evening readers, and 6 millions on Sundays. There seems in these degenerate days to be no way of frustrating it.

We are going to see *The Green Goddess* this evening, and I shall have to hurry away to catch the 11 p.m. train at Euston for Perth. I shall be back Sat. morning and hope to see you some time that day.

44 Bedford Square,

6th November, 1923.

I could not write to you yesterday, having only just time to rush from the Bonar Law funeral in Westminster Abbey. To me the most interesting thing about the funeral was the assembling of the pallbearers in Victoria Street. We were a very incongruous lot—P. of Wales, Carson, myself, Balfour, Baldwin, plus the only one who, I suppose, in his inmost depths was profoundly moved—Beaverbrook. The actual service in the Abbey was simple and good : when it was over, Baldwin asked me to give him a lift in the Royce to Downing St.—which I did. I said to him in the course of our short drive : " I am just off to Dewsbury, where I must give you a *wang* to-night." He replied with complete complaisance : " More power to your elbow ! " You would like him—as I do—but if he (who has already lasted more than the 200 days which were allotted to Bonar Law's Premiership) is also to be buried in the Abbey, there will be an almost irresistible case for setting up a new National Valhalla. I have no personal interest in the matter, as you well know.

Margot went with me to Dewsbury, and we stayed in the typical villa of a more than prosperous local manufacturer. It was interesting to see that it was just one or perhaps two stages behind the Sefton Park standard. We had a first-rate meeting, at which for the first time my utterances were "broadcast" by the agency of a microphone. I rather enjoyed myself for once, as Free Trade is a topic in which I am quite at home, and *The Times* to-day has a full verbatim report. You might look at it.

I got back to a late lunch to-day, and am now about to grapple (for a reasonable fee) with Winston's book. I hope to get to The Wharf Thursday—but it may be not till Friday.

44 Bedford Square,

7th November, 1923.

I was delighted to get your letter, and more than glad that you were pleased with my speech, which was for once well reported. It seems to have had a great success, and has not only astonished the Browns, but (what is more to the point under present conditions) perturbed the Baldwins.

I am so sorry about your throat : it is a good thing that you have Quiller-Couch for a bedside or sofa-side companion, when the brush is compulsorily laid aside.

ὁ συνοπτικὸς διαλεκτικὸς is to be found in the 7th book of Plato's *Republic* in a famous passage. It describes the final stage of a perfect education, when the youth has brought his piece-meal studies into a connected whole. For it is only—says Socrates—when you have attained to a *general* view of men and things and nature (σύνοψις) that you become capable of asking and answering questions, and of giving a real ground for what you think and believe. One who can do that is διαλεκτικὸς.

I am hard at it now at my review of Winston's second volume. I am working against time, as my first instalment must be ready by to-morrow (Thursday) evening. I shall come back some time on Friday for Puffin's 21st birthday. I shall see you Saturday, with a busy week in front : the House of Commons Tuesday, and two speeches, one at Walsall, the other in London, on Wed. and Thurs. What a life !

All blessings.

FERGUSLIE PARK,
PAISLEY,

21st November, 1923.

Thank you so much for your sweet letters. I am glad to hear that Anne is such a sturdy partisan.

In Dark Places is well worth reading though hardly, I think, as good as *The Pavement*.

We had a wonderfully good meeting last night [1] : the Town Hall packed full and much enthusiasm, and no kind of interruption. At present I have three opponents—all Labour : the familiar and three times defeated Biggar, an imported Communist solicitor called Cormack, who, if he persists, as I hope, in his candidature, will draw off from Biggar the Wild Men's votes, and a delightful old lunatic, Brown, who is over 70 and drives a cab in Paisley with a white horse, which he declares to be of Arab pedigree. I have a comparatively small district meeting to-night, and go

---

[1] On 22nd October Mr. Baldwin had declared that Protection of the Home Market was the only remedy for unemployment. His predecessor, Mr. Bonar Law, had given a pledge at the previous election that Protection, beyond certain " safeguarding " measures, would not be introduced. Mr. Baldwin therefore announced a dissolution of Parliament for 16th November, in order to secure a mandate.

to-morrow to Bradford, where I shall meet Margot and Violet, and return with them here on Friday. On Saturday Ll. G. and I hold our joint meeting, and exchange what was called in the French Revolution " le baiser de Lamourette."

I am very comfortably housed here : a typical millionaire villa with some Corots, a Sir Joshua, and a Hoppner intermixed with family photographs, and some sentimental Victorian mezzotints. It is a great improvement on the Central Hotel, and my host leaves me to myself.

FERGUSLIE PARK,
PAISLEY,

25th November, 1923.

You will understand why my letters have been so few and irregular. I was delighted to get yours with a glimpse of your experiences at *The Master Builder.* I have always thought it was the most impressively *actable* of Ibsen's plays. You don't tell me who did the woman : I have seen it done superbly by Elizabeth Robins.

When I got back on Friday evening I went to the Town Hall to a huge meeting, which had got rather out of hand under the oratory of Wedgwood Benn, and was developing distinct signs of turbulence. I succeeded in a few minutes in bringing them to heel (there was quite a number of cloth-capped Communists) and for half an hour (of rather dull discourse) you could have heard a pin drop.

Yesterday (Sat.) was, of course, the dramatic day. By way of preparing for the spectacular *rapprochement* in the evening, Violet and I went at 2.30 to a great football match—Paisley against the best of the Glasgow teams. It was too frosty and slippery for good football, but the sun shone, and there must have been between twenty and thirty thousand excited and obstreperous spectators. In our reserved row of stalls were Biggar, Cormack (the rival Labour candidate) and a new-comer, whom the Tories at the last moment have sprung upon us—one McInnes Shaw—son of a Glasgow Lord Provost. The local Tories didn't want to fight, and this stripling has been forced upon them from Headquarters. The whole thing is now a complex tangle, but we shall know better who the actual combatants at the poll will be after to-morrow (Monday), when the nominations have to be sent in.

At 7 o'clock Sat. evening the rites of Liberal Reunion were celebrated at an enthusiastic meeting in the Town Hall. Ll. G. arrived with his Megan, and I was accompanied by Margot and Violet. I have

84

rarely felt less exhilaration than when we got to the platform amid wild plaudits and a flash-light film was taken, " featuring " me and Ll. G. separated only by the chairman—an excellent local Doctor. I spoke for about quarter of an hour, and Ll. G. then plunged into a characteristic speech—ragged and boisterous, but with quite a good assortment of telling points. He was more than friendly and forthcoming, and the meeting was full of demonstrative fraternity. After it was over, Ll. G. and Megan, and their bodyguard of secretaries and detectives, were swept off by their host, Lord Maclay, to some baronial retreat, and we supped here in peace.

We all went this morning to the Coats' Memorial Church—a magnificent *Baptist* Cathedral which has been erected by the piety of his descendants to the memory of the founder of the great firm. It cost about £130,000, and I think was well worth it, for it is the finest modern specimen in Great Britain of the pure Early English style. Although what we should call a Nonconformist Chapel, there is a large surpliced choir of men, girls and boys, a wonderful organ, and the best singing I have heard for a long time. The sermon, too, was miles above the English standard.

Margot has driven into Glasgow to sustain and stimulate at an afternoon meeting her brother, Jack Tennant, who has chivalrously undertaken to contest the Central Division of that inconstant city. He hasn't the shadowiest ghost of a chance of being anywhere but at the bottom of the poll. And what makes it worse is that the campaign in the Central division has become one of organised rowdyism on all sides, with the result that none of the Candidates is allowed to finish more than two sentences.

So far here in Paisley the Labourites have behaved very well, and I have never been interrupted. I have a pretty bad week before me, leaving early to-morrow (Monday) morning for Nottingham—a journey which takes almost the whole day—and returning here on Tuesday at an equal expenditure of time, for two small evening meetings at Paisley. On Thursday I go to Alderley for the night for a big meeting at Manchester on Friday. Back here on Sat., and shall be a fixture here till polling day—the following Thursday.

As you say, the whole thing is a colossal (and tissue-wearing) gamble. I never felt more in doubt about the general result.

Halicarnassus ! I feel inclined to parody the familiar hymn, " Jerusalem, my happy home "—in some such fashion as this :

> " O Carian town, my would-be home,
>   Name ever dear to me,
>   When shall my labours have an end,
>   Thy joys, when shall I see ? "

86

During the sermon this morning my attention wandered to the High-Church clay-crabs,[1] and I thought out the enclosed which may amuse you.

I hope this long screed has not wearied you.

Blessings, etc.

FERGUSLIE PARK,
PAISLEY,

28th November, 1923.

You have been an angel in writing so regularly. I hope you got a fat letter which I sent you from here on Sunday.

My expedition to and from Nottingham was a terrific affair. I was eight or nine hours in the train each day Monday and Tuesday, and late for one of my meetings here last night in consequence of the fog. The Nottingham meeting was one of the most remarkable we have had. There were computed to be 10,000 people in the two halls and outside in the street. We shall do well if at the poll we can secure two of the seats there : the principal trade, lace-making, is very depressed, as they wrongly think from foreign competition, but really more from changes of fashion and

---

[1] Amanda Ros often alluded to clergymen, priests, etc., as " Christless clay-crabs."

87

lack of brains and enterprise. An import duty will do them no good.

I got back after a most wearisome journey only just in time for the second of my small meetings. There was a large infusion of Communists in the audience, who threatened to be very unruly, and from time to time unfurled a large red banner inscribed " Hail, Bolshevist Russia." Before I arrived they had been singing " The Red Flag," but they listened to me quietly, then asked a number of mostly silly questions amidst much general uproar. I have got two more meetings to-night.

To-morrow we go to Alderley for the night, and the next day, Friday, I have my final meeting in the Free Trade Hall at Manchester. I come back to Paisley Sat. morning and shall be here on Thursday. I find some relief at night from the strain of my daily life in two new P. G. Wodehouses. Thank God— there is only another week to polling.

FERGUSLIE PARK,
PAISLEY,

2nd December, 1923.

I have been living the life of a dog : much of it wasted in long railway journeys.

Some of the papers seem to have been giving picturesque and distorted accounts of disturbances at our meeting here. I have never been better listened to, and though we have had a lot of on the whole not unfriendly heckling, and once the demonstration I told you of with the Red Bolshevik banners, there has been nothing to complain of. Glasgow is quite different.

I went on Thursday with Margot and the faithful Basil to Alderley, which is near Manchester, and spent the night there with the Sheffields. Old Lord S.[1] (aged 85) is a marvel, and addresses two or three meetings every day in support of the candidature of his eldest son (Arthur) who is laid aside by (of all things) the mumps. Sir Hugh Bell—Lady S.'s brother, who is the doyen of the coal and iron trades, also arrived after speaking at two meetings for his nephew. He is a stripling of 80, as persistent in vitality as his brother-in-law, and the only man in England who can talk him down. They are a wonderful pair of veterans, and when we went to bed were indulging in a violent and verbose controversy as to the imports of foreign " pigs " (pig-iron) and Chinese lace. What will be left of the young men whom we see when they have attained three score years and ten, if they ever do ? The more I see of the successive generations the more I admire the Victorians.

[1] Lord Sheffield.

We have now, thank God, entered on the last lap—only three days more—and, except for a small function at Glasgow to-morrow, I shall be in Paisley till all is over. They are quite confident that I shall win, as I ought to, with two Labour antagonists. But we are wisely leaving nothing to chance. Buckmaster is coming on Wednesday. I have been going through the general list of candidates, and I cannot for the life of me see how we are going to come back more than 200 strong, it may be less.[1] Labour is the dark horse. The result which I should welcome would be that we should exceed Labour, and Baldwin find himself with a majority of 30 to 40—useless for his purpose, but

---

[1] The results of the election were :

					New Parliament.	At Dissolution.
Conservatives	.	.	.	.	285	346
Labour	.	.	.	.	191	144
Liberals	.	.	.	.	158	117
Independents	.	.	.	8	8

The Paisley figures were :

H. H. Asquith (L.)	.	.	.	.	.	9,723
J. M. Biggar (Lab.)	.	.	.	.	.	7,977
A. B. M. Shaw (U.)	.	.	.	.	.	7,758
D. D. Cormack (Lab.)	.	.	.	.	.	3,685

On 18th December, at a meeting of Liberal members at the National Liberal Club, Mr. Asquith declared that he would not keep the Conservatives in power ; and on 15th January, he supported the Labour amendment to the Address in the House of Commons, which in effect made Mr. Ramsay MacDonald Prime Minister.

sufficient to compel him to go on with the Government.

Anyway we shall come back on Friday and go to The Wharf Saturday, when at last I shall see you again.

I find Wodehouse a great stand-by ; *A Damsel in Distress* is excellently distracting. The Minister in his sermon to-day quoted ten lines from Browning's " Bishop Blougram's Apology," which you should read again. I am afraid that a chorus ending from Euripides would not disturb the complacency of the Paisley " bodies."

This will be my last letter from here—except a fragment or two.

Blessings untold, etc.

THE WHARF,

26th December, 1923.

It was a great joy to get your letter yesterday, Christmas Day. I thought it was rather in a low key —not unnaturally, for sunless snow in a Swiss hotel, peopled by provincials, is not calculated to raise one's spirits. These are our " crosses, Mr. Wesley."

We got well through the rigours of Christmas Day yesterday. We had a magnificent tree of 12 ft. high in the Mill House, well equipped with candles and all manner of coloured balls. There were only three grandchildren here—Cressida, Laura, and Priscilla : happily they get on well together. The technique of the tree was carefully looked after by tried veterans—Mikky,[1] Satterthwaite, and Sunburst.[2]

The weather here is vile—sunless, raw, and drizzling.

I assume that you get our papers—*The Times*, etc. If not, I will see that they are sent to you.

44 BEDFORD SQUARE,

1st February, 1924.

I looked in at Burlington House, where there is an exhibition of portraits—nearly 300 : on the whole a deplorably bad show, except for Orpen's Bishop of Ripon and a man by Fiddes Watt, which I thought the best things there.

Mostyn is busy to-day plying the Royce in the highways and byways of the City, to bring the faithful to

[1] Roderick Meiklejohn.   [2] Major Horace Crawfurd.

vote for Bell. It has been quite a lively election, and tho' I fear he won't get in, he will do much better than any Liberal has for the last fifty years.

I shall drive down to The Wharf after lunch to-morrow. Elizabeth is coming for her last Sunday : also Miss Sands the artist, who told me that she was a great friend and admirer of Dobbie. She is a clever woman.

I am getting swarms of resolutions from Liberal Associations all over the country expressing gratitude, etc. : a change from my correspondence of the last few weeks.

44 BEDFORD SQUARE,

5th February, 1924.

Thank you for your letter. Your description of the stupendous model is almost lyrical.

Lord Crewe, who is here from Paris for a few days, came to lunch, and I had a good though interrupted talk with him about the outlook in France. He is coming to resume it to-morrow. Augustus John also came ; he has just had his last sitting for Elizabeth's portrait. He says she is an exceptionally difficult model. She is wearing for it my beautiful old white Spanish mantilla, which the Queen of Portugal gave me years ago. John is a strange creature : I don't find it easy to penetrate his real being : he spoke very well of Dobbie, and regrets the folly of the Cardiff people in rejecting his design.

Miss Sands told me that Queen Victoria, who was latterly *éprise* with Disraeli, one day asked him what was his real religion. " Madam," he replied, " I am the blank page between the Old Testament and the New."

Whom is *The Gentlemen of China* by ? I had not heard of it. I have been reading rather disconnected odds and ends.

I shall see you Thursday.

44 Bedford Square,

14*th February*, 1924.

I was much interested in your account of the *Hamlet* performance. I am glad our Giles [1] came out of the ordeal so well. I have never in all my life seen a really good Hamlet : indeed the least unsatisfactory

[1] Gyles Isham.

was the accomplished but uninspired Forbes-Robertson. The rest of your cast do not seem from the critiques to have amounted to very much.

I dined at Grillion's last night—where there are often only half a dozen present. It was (as it turned out) a record in the history of the Club—now over 100 years old—both in number and quality of attendance. I have jotted down for your amusement the names of those who were present on the enclosed list. I sat next George Curzon, who is very good company, and I took the opportunity of opening up the subject of the Ruskin School Appeal. He was quite well disposed.

There is a good deal of excitement in the political world to-day over Poplar, which has brought into activity a hornets' nest. I suppose we could, if we liked, force a political crisis—the last thing I want to do, as far the best policy both for the country and for us is to give the Labour Government a free and full rope. Poor Ramsay—who looks every day more and more like a ghost—is suffering from neuritis, one of the most painful and disabling of afflictions, and has taken on a burden far too heavy for a man who is not (like me) composed, in equal proportions, of iron and leather, to carry for long. It is a pity; for, if he has to go on to the shelf there is none of his colleagues who could take his place.

Some of the family are coming to dinner to-night. And I am now going down to the House (it is an early Friday sitting) to cast a rather reluctant vote for local option in Wales !

I hope to see you in blooming looks on Sunday.

HOUSE OF COMMONS,

4th March, 1924.

As Margot was going to a Spanish Fête yesterday evening, I thought I would sample *The Way of the World*. I regret to say I found it very disappointing. It is a bad play with a lot of witty dialogue, and a silly involved plot. Or rather a tangle of situations which come to nothing. Every character is more than odious. The costumes and *décor* are quite good, but the dialogue is slurred and blurred by almost all the actors. The much-belauded Edith Evans is quite a good actress, and I should like to see her in a real part. I thought the best of the cast were Robert Loraine and Nigel Playfair himself, who was the only one who spoke the words really well. I see from the biographies that it was the last and least successful of Congreve's plays : he would never write for the stage again.

I went to lunch to a great function at "Amen House," close to Paternoster Row, to celebrate the opening of the new quarters of the Oxford University Press. There was a most distinguished gathering of Oxford and some Cambridge High Brows, and it was a much more satisfactory and entertaining function than the Union Banquet. The Archbishop of Canterbury made a rather dreary speech. The only other speakers were Curzon and myself, and Arthur Balfour, who responded for the University of Cambridge. He was in excellent form and chaffed Oxford and glorified Cambridge in his best style. I sat next my old friend the Bishop of Ripon and the new Oxford Vice-Chancellor, Wells, the Warden of Wadham, whom I found an agreeable companion.

The House is as dull as can be.

Blessings,

H.

HOTEL DE L'HERMITAGE,
MONTE CARLO,

Easter Monday, April 1924.

I was delighted to get your news. Our weather here is perfect : sunshine all day and a nice nip in the

air when one gets above sea-level. We take long
drives among the hills—fine steep grey rocks going up
almost to the snow line, and penetrated by marvellously engineered roads.

My travelling companions are very considerate, and
leave me as much as I like to myself. Lady S. is a
very good sort, with a large fund of sense and shrewd-
ness.

I read in my sitting-room in the sun in the morning
—also at night. I have been going through the 5th
and 6th vols. of Buckle's *Life of Disraeli*, with a view
to my book. What a man! Mrs. Dizzy throughout
their married life always cut his hair. On her death
(at over 80) he took up with Selina (aged 55) and her
sister Anne (aged 70), both grandmothers, and during
the last eight years of his life wrote Selina a thousand
letters, let alone those which are not preserved. It is
a pathetic business, because it is clear that she never
cared for him, but was vain of his unconcealed admiration, and fond of getting to know State secrets
before other people. About mid-way in their friendship (1877) he writes to her : " Gussie has asked me to
dine there on Sunday—to meet you. It is exactly
four years ago that I met you dining at that very house
—four years ago ! It makes one very sad. I gave
you feelings you could not return. It was not your
fault : my fate and my misfortune." I have no fond-

ness for the man, who possessed some of the qualities which I hate most. But when I read this again I could not keep the tears from my eyes. He had sound ideas about the tribe of doctors, who mismanaged him shamefully. " They are all alike," he says. " First of all they throw it on the weather : then there must be a change of scene : so Sir W. Jenner, after blundering and plundering in the usual way, sent me to Bournemouth, and Gull wants to send me to Ems. I should like to send both of them to Jericho."

It was only the old quack Kidd who, in the end, gave him some relief. One cannot but be thankful that at the same time of life one is not racked by recurrent gout and asthma.

HOTEL DE L'HERMITAGE,

MONTE CARLO,

25th April, 1924.

I can't tell you how much I enjoyed reading your last letter. You have been keeping your eyes open to your surroundings, and I have not for a long time read a more vivid description of what an English village looks like to those who have eyes to see. The feudal lady in the grey stone house, the fetid over-crowded cottages, the snarling fathers, the complacent curate—

what a picture ! I don't wonder that you felt that we are up against colossal things. To talk to such people of the sanctities of marriage and the delights of home is a mockery ; and yet, if you were to try to infuse a disturbing spark into the " clod," after at the most a momentary smouldering it would be smothered out. It seems sometimes a desperate business : as Priscilla says, " a circle that leads nowhere." You at any rate had the sun to shine on you.

I was sad at the death of our dear Corelli [1] : you and I had such good times in her company. Duse too ! How lucky that there was a chance of seeing her last year.

This is the last letter that I shall write from here : I hope to be at Bedford Square Monday afternoon. Being here has done me real good, but it is becoming a trifle monotonous.

44 Bedford Square,
London,

6th May, 1924.

We had a useful two hours in the House yesterday over the Eviction Bill, when the Tory-Labour com-

[1] Marie Corelli.

bination climbed down, and our Liberal Bill sailed safely into haven. The Manchester Simon (Sir John's namesake, but no connection) has distinguished himself over this.

One is apt to be pessimistic in these dark times (as you and I were on Sunday), but this may interest you written (two years before I was born) on New Year's Day 1850 by Dizzy to Count d'Orsay :

" England is only sinking. France is finished. What a mournful fate to be born in the decline and fall of great countries ! Europe—at least the Europe of our fathers and our youth—approaches its end. We ought to have formed our careers across the great waters."

He always struck a falsetto note. The " great waters " means (I suppose) the Atlantic. But which of us at this moment would desire to have been born, or adopted and acclimatised, as an American ?

I go by motor to Chelmsford to-morrow (Wed.) afternoon, and, after speaking there in the evening, come back here by midnight. I am wonderfully strong and well. But I miss you always and everywhere.

44 BEDFORD SQUARE,

13th May, 1924.

We went to a huge full-dress banquet in honour of the Rumanians at the Palace last night : about 120 guests, all arrayed like Solomon in his glory. I sat next Mrs. Davidson, the Arch-Bishopess of Canterbury, who is a nice woman and, considering that she is the daughter of one Archbishop and the wife of another and has spent her whole life in a clerical atmosphere, is amazingly broadminded and free from the prejudices and jargon of the profession. I talked with the two Kings—ours and the Rumanian—and was rather favourably impressed with the latter : but you never know from their conversation and manners here what foreign royalties are in their own homes. The Queen, who used to be a great charmer, has still distinct traces of beauty and is really intelligent. We had to go to another function to-day, where they were received at the Guildhall by the Lord Mayor and Corporation of London : always a highly picturesque ceremony : I remember one of the same kind in honour of the German Emperor sixteen years ago. Happily the King was content with a very brief speech in excellent English.

44 BEDFORD SQUARE,

24th June, 1924.

We went (Margot, Puffin and I) to a really good thing last night : Arnold Bennett's *The Great Adventure*, which I had not seen since before the war. It is of course a real farce from first to last, but it amuses almost the whole time, and the two principal parts were quite admirably played by Leslie Faber and Hilda Trevelyan : as good, both of them, as we can now get on the English stage. It gave me more pleasure than anything I have seen this year since *The Green Goddess*. Being not at all pro-Bennett, I was surprised at the excellence of the dialogue.

Margot went again with the " boys "—Puff, Hartley and Co.—this afternoon to Wembley, which is the prevailing passion.

To-morrow I have rather an exacting day, as I have to go to a function at the London Hospital, then to look in at the House, and for a few moments to the Palace Garden Party, and after dinner (if I am in the mood) I shall hear the new prodigy Giannini, about whom all the critics rave and who is singing at an American party.

I am delighted that in the Golf Open Championship at Hoylake the veteran J. H. Taylor, who won his first championship more than thirty years ago, is so far easily ahead of all competitors.

44 BEDFORD SQUARE,

8th July, 1924.

We had a little brush in the House with the chaotically confused statement of Ramsay M. Much more interesting was the Dr. Clifford demonstration at Westminster Chapel : a crowd of about 3,000, for the most part Nonconformist *bourgeoisie.* I spoke for about a quarter of an hour and was followed by Ll. G. who was really picturesque and interesting, without being too flamboyant—quite an artistic performance.

Dennis Eadie came to lunch with his author Munroe, who wrote *Mrs. Beam,* and is now producing with him another play, which Eadie says is better and happily includes in the cast Jean Cadell.

As there is nothing of any interest in the House to-day, we are going to look in at Gerald Du Maurier's garden party at Hampstead.

44 BEDFORD SQUARE,

11th July, 1924.

You would have enjoyed the Du Maurier garden party ; more than the one I had to go to last night at Wimborne House, where after dinner I must have shaken hands with some 2,000 men and women : mainly good Liberals, but with a sprinkling of Ambassadors like the Italian and the German, and some literary folk. It is incredible that people, with more or less immortal souls, should find these gatherings amusing. But the appetite for them is apparently insatiable, and there were all the outward signs of successful pleasure hunting. Our hostess, Lady Wimborne, behaved like a heroine : she got up out of bed, where she had been for five days with a temperature of 103, and after a long dinner stood for an hour and a half shaking hands. She is a charming creature.

I have spent the morning trying to put together some things to say at Norwich, whither I start almost immediately. I am glad that this is the last for the present of my " campaigning " speeches in the country.

44 BEDFORD SQUARE,

31st October, 1924.

You sent me the sweetest of letters, with one of the gems of the Anthology.

We had cheering crowds at the railway stations, both at Glasgow at the start and at Euston at the finish, of our journey yesterday.[1] I have had whole budgets of telegrams and letters to-day from all sorts and conditions of people almost in all parts of the world. Some of them are really touching, and quite a lot come from political opponents. Lord Stam-

---

[1] On Oct. 8th, 1924, "the Conservatives moved a Vote of Censure on the Labour Government for having, on political grounds and on account of pressure exerted by back bench Labour members, dropped the prosecution of the Editor of the *Worker's Weekly* for seditious libel. The Liberal Party moved an amendment to the Vote of Censure, calling for a Select Committee of Enquiry. This amendment the Prime Minister, Mr. Ramsay MacDonald, speaking the night before at the Queen's Hall, had called 'a vote of censure conceived in a spirit of mediæval crookedness and torture.' In the Debate he refused to accept such a Committee of Enquiry, and insisted upon treating the proposal as a Vote of Censure. The amendment was carried by 364 votes to 198, and on the following day the Prime Minister announced the Dissolution of Parliament." Mr. Asquith's speech, following that of the Prime Minister, was his last in the House of Commons, for he lost his seat at Paisley. The figures were : E. R. Mitchell (Lab.) 17,057, H. H. Asquith (L.) 14,829.

fordham and E. Grey and Pamela came to lunch. Stamfordham brought a nice message from the King.

Oc is pressing me to go with him to Egypt, whither he starts on his annual visit in the course of the next fortnight. I am rather tempted to do so, as it would secure a few weeks of welcome change, and I should really like to see the country.

We seem to have polled over 3 million votes, which is not bad for a dying party set between the upper and nether millstones. Ll. G. is coming to see me in the morning.

44 BEDFORD SQUARE,

5th November, 1924.

Yesterday was a divine day from first to last. I look back upon every moment and wish it could return.

I got here in time for our conclave, which was attended by about a dozen. Ll. G. was at first very intractable, and seemed bent on mischief. He evidently thinks that over forty M.P.s are for the most part his men, and there was a good deal of friction between him and Simon and D. Maclean. He quieted down in time and became more reasonable. In the end we arranged to have meetings of the M.P.s and afterwards of the rejected candidates next

Monday, both to be addressed by me. I shall have to think over these allocutions rather carefully, and I have written to Lynam putting off my discourse to the Dragons until my return, when I will speak to them about Egypt.

I had a very nice letter from the King, full of regrets and gratitude. He says that he " feels strongly that I should not be subject to further political contests, nor the exacting, wearing life of the House of Commons." So he offers me off his own bat a Peerage, so that I could continue my " parliamentary life under more peaceful conditions "—adding, " if I could persuade you to do this it would give me great pleasure." I will show it you on Friday. It was very tactful and kind of him to write in the interregnum between two Governments : so that it would be entirely his own proposal.

MILAN, EN ROUTE TO (TRIESTE),

13th November, 1924.

I take advantage of a short halt here to send you a few lines, which I may be able to have posted at Trieste or Venice. I went to lunch with Marthe [1] at Elizabeth's and Antoine's flat in the Quai Bourbon.

[1] Princess Marthe Bibesco.

I had never seen it before. It is well placed close to Notre-Dame, on a promontory projecting into the river, which laps it on three sides. It is quite small—only two effective sitting-rooms, or at the outside three, and all of them on rather a miniature scale. I was rather disappointed with Antoine's pictures ; he parted some time ago with his two Cézannes : and an excessive area of the very limited wall space is taken up with two very big things by Vuillard, who was one of the pioneers and is still a " Master " among the Post-Impressionists. They are quite clever, but it would bore me to have them always there ; they are like tapestry.

Marthe is a clever woman who, despite the ravages of six months of serious operations with all sorts of complexities, retains her looks and her *joie de vivre*. She still has to walk with a stick, but she took me with much agility over Notre-Dame, and what is said to be the oldest church in Paris—St. Julien des Pauvres. The first I know pretty well, but was glad to see it again : the two Rose windows in the transept are the finest in all the Gothic cathedrals. The other is quite interesting—Romanesque, contemporary with our Norman, with round arches and thick, dignified columns with striking capitals.

All to-day's railway journey by the banks of the Lake of Geneva and through the Simplon tunnel, past

Lake Maggiore, has been over familiar ground. Between here and Venice we shall pass my favourite Lago di Garda. The little Italian soldiers stationed —rarely more than 5 ft. 2 inches in height—look like sturdy marionettes. This (Lombardy) is the most anti-Mussolini part of Italy.

I am just going to begin the much-commended novel—*The Constant Nymph*.

The weather, which was execrable in Paris, brightens as we get further south. We get to Trieste at midnight, and to-morrow I shall start on my three days' sea voyage.

THE BRITISH CONSULATE-GENERAL,
BEYROUT,

1st December, 1924.

I think it was from Jerusalem that I last wrote to you. I have seen some famous scenes—Biblical and otherwise—since then. My travelling companion has been a young Cust, who is on the staff at Jerusalem and is a cousin of my old friend Harry. He is an intelligent young man and speaks French and Arabic (the two necessary languages in these parts) fluently. He saves me all the minor troubles of travelling, and is quite a pleasing comrade.

The weather has been splendid ever since we left the Holy City ; bright sun all day and very little wind, though it is mid-winter here. We had a good drive to Shechem (much mentioned in the Old Testament)—one of the many places where the body of St. John the Baptist is buried. His head is said to be beneath a shrine (which we saw later) in the centre of the principal Mosque in Damascus ; for he is a Moslem as well as a Christian saint. The most interesting sight at Shechem (now called Nablus) is the dwindling remnants of the sect of Samaritans ; about 120 men, women and children all told. They are Hebrews who loathe the Jews just as much as the Jews loathe them—as in the days of the Good Samaritan and the Woman of Samaria. I went to their squalid little chapel in a kind of rabbit burrow, where they keep some rare MSS. of the Pentateuch and some fine vestments. The Arch Priest had actually paid a visit to London. All the men are priests, who do nothing for a living, but distil illicit spirits on a small scale, and as there is only a handful of women, the race is within sight of extinction. They seemed to me to be nice, quiet people.

Thence we went on to Nazareth, the Lake of Tiberias, and Capernaum. These places are of course all in Galilee, which is a much more attractive district than Judæa. Nazareth contains a lot of mythical

" objects of interest "—the place where the Virgin
received the Annunciation and the actual Incarnation
began, the carpenter's shop, etc., etc. It is a very
picturesque village, and the women—some of them
quite good-looking—coming at sunset to the well, and
carrying back on their heads their huge jars full of
water, tilted at an acute angle, without spilling a drop
or raising a finger, give me the sense that East is
East. Tiberias is the only beautiful bit of scenery that
I have come across in the Holy Land. It is a good-
sized lake about 12 miles long, with deep blue water,
sheer cliffs on one side and trees and gardens on the
other, with a fine view in the background of the snowy
top of Mount Hermon, which though well outside
Palestine is a conspicuous landmark. There are very
few " little ships on the sea," as the children's hymn
says—which is subject to sudden storms. The place
swarms with Jews (unlike Nazareth which is full of
Christians), and we were told that a jutting point with
a fine wood had been purchased by Sir Alfred Mond
as a site for a winter villa.

We had a long railway journey to Damascus and
spent yesterday (Sunday) in a trip from there to
Baalbec. Damascus is a far more beautiful town and
much fuller of interest than anything in Palestine, and
Baalbec is I suppose the most stupendous ruin in the
world. I must tell you about these in another letter.

I am writing this en route to Egypt. I hope to be again in Cairo on Wednesday, December 3rd. How you would love being here.

THE CATARACT HOTEL,
ASSOUAN,

Sunday, 14th December, 1924.

I was delighted to get your letter of November 28th. So London is at last to be enriched with a nude statue. I am glad that Mr. Bretherton appreciates your drawing, but I can hardly imagine less attractive or repaying models for your pencil than the members of the present Cabinet, from Baldwin himself down to Sir " Jix " and Sir " Worthy " and the rest of his unremembered baronets.

I spent the greater part of last week at Luxor, where and in the neighbourhood is to be found the *crème de la crème* of the old Egyptian tombs and temples. I had a learned antiquarian as guide and interpreter and an excellent little dragoman recommended by Oc, who goes by the name of " Billy Joseph." The weather, as seems always to be the case at this time of the year, was perfect, and not at all too hot. The sight-seeing, which I did pretty thoroughly, was rather fatiguing work, as there are long series of underground steps and galleries to be traversed before you reach the ultimate resting-places of the Kings. They were haunted all their lives—not without reason—with the dread of tomb plunderers, and their architects showed fiendish ingenuity in trying to put these gentry off the scent. It was all-important to the future of the dead man that the magnificent offerings that were buried with him should be kept intact for consumption and use by Osiris and the other underground gods, and his own double or *Ka*. The real interest of Tutankhamen's tomb is that it is almost the only one that has been left unrifled.

Some of the wall paintings and reliefs are really wonderful works of art, and as fresh as they were 3,000 years ago ; but one gets tired of the monotony and conventionality with which the same subjects are treated generation after generation. It is the same with the great temples ; there must be even now, when so much has been destroyed, something between fifty and a hundred statues of a single Pharaoh—Rameses II, whose yoke was so heavy on the Hebrews. Both in imagination and workmanship the oldest of what is left seems to me to be far the best. I left Luxor on Friday and came on here, about 130 miles further south. The hotel is on even a more gigantic scale than that at Luxor, but is not more than a quarter full. Assouan is in itself a more attractive place than Luxor. The river narrows almost into a gorge and is full of rocky inlets, which form the beginning of what is called the First Cataract. There are not many tombs or temples, Philæ being the only one of much account, but the situation is really beautiful ; a welcome change to the generally featureless banks of the Nile. It is a delightful resting-place, and I have taken up my book and hope to make some progress with it before I leave (on the 20th) for Khartoum, where I shall rejoin Oc. I expect we shall be back home about the middle of January.

KHARTOUM,
SUDAN,

Christmas Eve, 1924.

Since I last wrote I have spent the best part of a week at Assouan, which is much the pleasantest place in Egypt for a stay. The hotel is on a gigantic scale and overlooks what is called the First Cataract, where for the first time the Nile becomes beautiful as a river ; it was three-quarters empty, and I lived in great comfort and perfect peace. I used to sit in my room in the morning and work at my book. I must have written about 14,000 words while I was there and no one ever disturbed me. Unlike Luxor, it is not a centre for seeing tombs and temples, though there are two or three interesting features—perhaps the most so a gigantic obelisk, such as we see in front of all the temples, still lying in its quarry, with the underside not yet detached. It is still an unsolved mystery how, with no better tools than wedges and chisels and rollers, they hewed out and moved these monstrous monoliths to enormous distances, and then set them on their ends and covered them with hieroglyphics and reliefs. Mr. Watt, who looks after the great dam at Assouan, kindly lent me his launch, in which I used to cruise up and down the river every afternoon. My companion was generally the local doctor—Dr. N., an Australian, who is a great friend of Parkie's and knows the whole region and all its people intimately. I saw something too of "Watson Pasha," who used to be Kitchener's aide-de-camp and general factotum in all his earlier campaigns.

I was sorry to leave, and embarked on Saturday evening on a Sudan steamer (the Government insisting on treating me as their guest) on a voyage south for the best part of two days and nights, to Wady Halfa, where the Sudan proper begins. It was quite a pleasant experience, as the weather was perfect, and I chatted from time to time with some officers of the East Lancashire regiment who were bringing up a detachment of their men to strengthen the garrison at Khartoum. I took the train at Halfa, and a few stations further on was joined by Oc, who came on with me to Khartoum, and will again be my companion after this. We are staying in a very nice house on the river belonging to the Schusters : he is Finance Minister here and his wife is a particularly nice woman. We go on for Christmas Day to Barakat, where are the headquarters of Oc's Syndicate, and from there shall visit the great Gezireh dam, returning here at the end of the week.

I suppose you will be spending your Christmas in your new handiwork—The Foundry. All blessings be with you and it. But you would like being with me here in this wonderful climate where the sun shines all day and it is never (so far) too hot. The desert through which we travelled for 200 miles is most impressive.

44 BEDFORD SQUARE,

27th January, 1925.

Thank you for your delightful letter. I was very glad to be reminded of Dr. J's description of the Rev.

Prebendary Zachariah Mudge. I turned it up when I read your extract in Boswell. The Doctor appears never to have published it, at any rate with his name, but showed it to Sir Joshua when it was written. It is a marvellous example of his style when at its best—and worst.[1] Northcote seems to have said of it to Hazlitt, in one of his Conversations later in life, that " it is like one of Kneller's portraits—it would do for anybody." Sir Joshua's Latin quotation is from the *Ars Poetica* of Horace and means : " He takes the first prize who has been able to mix the Useful and Agreeable—at once delighting and admonishing his reader " : said of poetry not painting ; but a priggish rule at the best.

[1] " The Reverend Mr. Zachariah Mudge, Prebendary of Exeter, and Vicar of St. Andrew's in Plymouth ; a man equally eminent for his virtues and abilities, and at once beloved as a companion and reverenced as a pastor. He had the general curiosity to which no kind of knowledge is indifferent or super-fluous ; and that general benevolence by which no order of men is hated or despised, etc."

The passage which probably struck Lord Oxford as so char-acteristic is the concluding paragraph of the portrait : " The grandeur and solemnity of the preacher did not intrude upon his general behaviour ; at the table of his friends he was a companion communicative and attentive, of unaffected manners, of manly cheerfulness, willing to please and easy to be pleased. His acquaintance was universally solicited, and his presence ob-structed no enjoyment which religion did not forbid. Though studious, he was popular ; though argumentative, he was modest ; though inflexible, he was candid ; and though metaphysical, yet orthodox."

Don't change your mode of address for another week. I get sheaves of letters by every post : I will show you some of them : they come often from the most unexpected quarters, e.g. Barrie, Henson the Bishop of Durham, Mr. Marchant of the Goupil, Clarkson the wigmaker, and Mrs. Kendal the *doyenne* of the Stage. I had an amusing one this morning from Lindsay, the Master of Balliol, who tells me that in the war his General was quite unimpressed by the fact that he was a Fellow of Balliol, until one day they came on Beb [1] in an ammunition dump. Lindsay (who was his contemporary) greeted him and was asked by the General how he knew him. He told him, and added that he had tutored another of my sons (Cys). The General : " But I thought they were very clever fellows." Lindsay : " So they are." General : " Then *you* must be a devil of a swell ! " I am overwhelmed with correspondence.

All blessings.

44 BEDFORD SQUARE,
4th February, 1925.

Thank you so much for your letter. I made some progress with *The Rector's Daughter* last night, and have

[1] Herbert Asquith.

just come to the point where Herbert succumbs to the rather obvious charmer Kathy. Neither of them interests me, but the Canon and Mary are both marvellously drawn. I think the writing of the book very good—vivid and yet restrained. Goonie Churchill,[1] who dined here last night, says that Birrell prefers it to the *Nymph*.

I feel sorry that poor old John Lane has dropped out of the ranks, though the last time we saw him I thought he seemed frail and incapable of holding on. The obituaries in the papers depict him as a mutineer and pioneer—which is exactly the impression he would most have liked to leave behind him. He certainly didn't *chasser de race* : for there was nothing in him which suggested a Quaker stock.

I went into the National Gallery for half an hour before lunch and discovered a quaint portrait by Tilly Kettle, and examined their only Manet—the Execution of the Emperor Maximilian of Mexico.

M. Venizelos has just been to lunch : rather a pathetic figure, for the Greece which he did so much to aggrandise is now in the trough of the waves ; and he tells me has to support on her own soil a million Greek refugees from Turkey.

[1] Lady Gwendoline Churchill.

44 BEDFORD SQUARE,

5th February, 1925.

At bedtime I persevere with *The Rector's Daughter.* I take it slowly—not from boredom but from quiet enjoyment ; and I have just crossed poor Mary's Rubicon, when the not very convincing clerical husband of Kathy folds Mary in his arms. I am glad not to know yet exactly what is going to happen, though I have surmises. I see some signs of decadence in the Canon, but I hope he will keep up his end to the last. Kathy, Lesbia and Co. are drawn with rather excessive crudeness : but it is undoubtedly a distinguished book.

I went last night to a dinner at Mrs. Keppel's : she showed herself a stout and loyal friend, when our fortunes seemed to be at a low ebb : and this is so rare that it fills one with lasting gratitude—especially at a time like this, when everyone (in apparent forgetfulness of what many thought and said in days gone by) is in a fawning mood.

This morning in my half-hour before lunch I revisited the Soane Museum in Lincoln's Inn Fields, which I have not seen for over twenty years. It is in its way most interesting, and we must go there together. Soane was a great architect ; he built the

Bank of England and was in his way both a fastidious and an omnivorous collector. Hogarth's eight pictures of the Rake's Progress are there : they cost Soane £200, and are now worth well over £20,000. It is a strange assortment (including one of the finest of all the Egyptian sarcophagi) and without any rubbish.

We are all going this evening to see *Just Married*. Margot and I drive down to The Wharf after the American dinner at midnight to-morrow.

44 BEDFORD SQUARE,

11th February, 1925.

You will see in the papers to-day the official announcement from the *Gazette*, which transforms my status, for better or for worse, but at any rate for good and all. Clouder[1] did his best to live up to the occasion, and his first "My Lord" had an unmistakable tinge of delicate courtliness. I got the official intimation when I returned here after driving from The Wharf last night—the 10th, and then I suddenly remembered that it was my Father's birthday : for he was born on the 10th of February 1825—exactly one

---

[1] Lord Oxford's butler.

hundred years ago to the day. What would the lovers of coincidence say to that?

We had a meeting at Abingdon St. this morning of our " Shadow " Cabinet. Ll. G. was there and E. Grey, with others. We had quite a good talk. At lunch we had amongst others Winston Churchill, who was in his best form : he is a Chimborazo or Everest among the sand-hills of the Baldwin Cabinet.

As Elizabeth is leaving on Wednesday, we have arranged to have my installation in the H. of Lords on Tuesday. You might come up for it. Balfour and Beauchamp are to be my two " supporters." I go to see the King to-morrow at noon. I have just got the enclosed which you might like to read—as it comes from one of the more reputable of the American papers. I come back to Wharf after lunch on Friday.

44 BEDFORD SQUARE,

12th February, 1925.

I am sad to hear that your neuralgia still worries and disables you. You must give your eyes a rest. I hope and believe that Monday's was not what Browning calls " the last ride together " of Mrs. H. and Mr. A.

I am spending odd moments in rummaging in my drawers, and find there in " admired confusion " old letters of by-gone years which I am trying to sort out into some kind of order. As a sample of the odd and unremembered things that have accumulated, I found two this morning from dear old Rhoda Broughton, written not long before her death.

I went to see the King this morning and spent the best part of an hour with him, chatting mainly over old days. He was more than kind and nice. À propos of double titles, Lord Aberdeen when we made him a Marquis took the names of " Aberdeen and Temair." Lady A. sent to a friend a photograph of herself with a Scotch terrier on her knee signed with the new style. The friend replied with effusive thanks, adding, " It was so nice, too, to see your little dog *Temair*." This was one of the King's anecdotes which made him roar with laughter. I drive down after lunch to-morrow.

All love.

44 BEDFORD SQUARE,

25th February, 1925.

I am so glad to hear that you are feeling better. How do you like *Dr. Thorne* ? It is not exciting, but there is in it a good deal of disguised art.

Barrymore came to lunch yesterday and we all liked him, but there is nothing magnetic or "dæmonic" about him. Priscilla left this morning for America : her father joins her at Cherbourg. She has certainly improved in manners and general amiability, and is a clever and attractive child, whom we shall miss. Elizabeth begins her rehearsals at Everyman's next Monday. She hopes to get Edith Evans and Marie Tempest into the cast.

Noel Coward of *The Vortex*, who spent Sunday at The Wharf two or three weeks ago, seems to have been disappointed. He was fool enough to say that he was accustomed to " shine " and not to be " shone at," and resented being sent to play " Nines " with the Governess and the Tutor ! (the Tutor being Bongie !).

I am just off to the House of Lords [1] to listen to a small debate. At present they only sit two days a week—rather a change after forty years of the other place.

Beau Geste is said to be a good novel. I must stop now with all love and blessings.

[1] Lord Oxford took his seat in the House of Lords on February 17th. His supporters were Lord Balfour and Lord Crewe.

44 BEDFORD SQUARE,
17th March, 1925.

The great event here yesterday was Elizabeth's play.[1] The little Everyman Theatre was crammed with what is called a " distinguished company," including all the critics from Walkley and Desmond downwards. I was rather anxious during the prolonged verbal conversations of the first act, but in the second we got down to real business, and the third was (without any exaggeration) fine and moving. There was quite an ovation at the fall of the curtain, and such critiques as I have read are friendly in tone. Of course the technique needs to be improved, and the " cackle " cut down. But there is much more sense of real drama in it than I had expected. Edith Evans' performance (with one or two flaws) was that of a great artist, and Cellier, who only gets his chance in the last act, rose to it and was quite impressive. Felix Aylmer also was first rate. Whether it will catch on for a run it is difficult to say.

Elizabeth gave a supper after at this house to all the cast (except Evans, who was too tired) and a number of others who included Viola Tree (very enthusiastic) and Diana Cooper.

All love and blessings.

[1] *The Painted Swan.*

126

44 BEDFORD SQUARE,

18th March, 1925.

Margot and Puffin went to the second night of *The Swan* yesterday, and said that it went better than the first. The house was crowded, and the advance " bookings " show that it will be well supported during its appointed fortnight at the Everyman. The idea is then to transplant it, for a further trial, to the Ambassadors, which, as you know, is quite a small playhouse, and becomes unfortunately vacant through the fiasco of Miss Tennyson Jesse's *Anyhouse.* On the whole the critics have been less fault-finding and more appreciative than I expected.

I dined with the Higgins, where I met Ruby and Buckmaster. I hope you are going strong with your painting.

Jack Beresford has sent me a book he has just brought out, a diary of an 18th-century clergyman called Woodforde. It is a chronicle of small beer, but it has a certain interest as a picture of village life and society in such counties as Somerset and Norfolk. All classes seem to have eaten and drunk much more than they do now : otherwise *plus ça change plus c'est la même chose.* I must go now to give my final sitting to Orde.

44 BEDFORD SQUARE,

20th March, 1925.

I don't quite know what your immediate movements are, but I assume you are going to the Foundry to meet your Dobbies to-morrow. I shall get to The Wharf in the course of the day and will come over and see you on Sunday morning.

Poor George Curzon died quietly at 5 this morning, after a fortnight of pain and constant restlessness. It is exactly a fortnight since I heard him speak in the House of Lords, apparently in full vigour, excellent form and high spirits. He was seven years younger than I am, and I have known him ever since I examined him, a schoolboy at Eton, very nearly fifty years ago. We entered the House of Commons in the same Election in 1886. It makes one feel, as Browning says in the *Toccata*, " chilly and grown old."

We had a nice actress here at lunch, Miss Muriel Pope, who plays an unsympathetic part in *The Swan*.

I looked in for ten minutes at the Goupil and grasped Mr. Marchant's hand. He has not got a good exhibition, but there are two sunlit views of Avignon by William Nicholson, and two also by John Nash, which are the best I have seen of his.

All blessings.

44 Bedford Square,

24th March, 1925.

We had a " full choral service " in honour of George Curzon in the House of Lords yesterday afternoon. I took some pains with the form of my little contribution, and it was well received.[1] The others I must say were limping, broken-backed, draggle-tailed compositions, which ought to have been turned down in any board school. Pomposity and idleness in combination deface our public speaking. So far, I have not heard (with the exception of poor Curzon's last) even a decent speech in the House of Lords.

Nan Tennant is going to accompany us in our trip to Provence. She is a sound, sensible woman and has a sense of humour : so I praise God for her.

The family (without me) went to see *Rose Marie* at Drury Lane last night and brought back a better report than I expected.

I am going as a pall-bearer to the Curzon funeral to-morrow morning and shall probably make a little speech about the House of Lords in the afternoon.

[1] It was his maiden speech in the House of Lords.

44 BEDFORD SQUARE,

25th March, 1925.

I went last night with Elizabeth and Puffin to the Tivoli, and saw two American films ; one, almost the best, and the other quite the worst, I have ever seen. It is a strange lottery.

We went to-day to George Curzon's funeral at Westminster Abbey : I was one of the pall-bearers. It was quite a simple ceremony, despite all the pomp and circumstance of the surroundings. The only person there I saw really moved was his old brother Frank, who sobbed behind me while the choir sang " Abide with me."

I am just going down to the H. of Lords, and may be moved to say a few words about the reform of the Second Chamber. It is a lovely day.

I fear I shall not see you till Saturday : I assume you are now at the Foundry more or less permanently.

All best blessings and dearest love.

44 BEDFORD SQUARE,

26th March, 1925.

I have only time for two or three lines. We had a rather scrambling debate in the Lords yesterday about a Second Chamber, in the course of which I gave tongue for a few minutes. The standard of speaking there is deplorably low : men like —— and —— and —— would hardly be listened to in an average County Council. They mumble away a lot of spineless and disconnected platitudes.

We had a new-comer—the Chief Justice Lord Hewart—to dinner last night : a self-made man, who began in the Press gallery, with a good deal of rough-hewn force and character. My two nice little sisters-in-law, Katherine and Nancy Tennant, came to lunch to-day. They are delightful girls, full of spirit and adventure, and have just come back from rambling over Greece and Dalmatia.

To-morrow night I go to a " complimentary " dinner at Lincoln's Inn, back at The Wharf by lunch-time Saturday.

BEDFORD SQUARE,

27th April, 1925.

It was a great joy to see you again in the new surroundings which you are erecting and making into a real home. You will have to be careful in safeguarding its amenities against the attractive Prendy and the possible ravages of his Comus crew.

After I left you I did not get much fun or profit out of my Sunday with its thunder clouds and peals. I drove up this morning with Elizabeth, and found myself soon immersed in prosaic realities, of which Godfrey Collins and Vivian Phillipps—who came to lunch—were for the moment the carnal impersonations. The Liberal " Million " fund takes a lot of getting on to its legs.

It is a rather lurid sign of the times that the Germans should have elected Hindenburg who represents what was worst in their past and is most dangerous for their future.

I am alone here : Violet and Bongie are coming to dinner.

All blessings,

H.

44 Bedford Square,

27th May, 1925.

A worse day for the Derby could hardly be imagined : it has not ceased to pour since day-break. I was careful not to predict the winner, and the only tip I gave was the Aga's Zionist for a place. He seems to have come in second, and a very bad second.

I went to the luncheon which they gave me at the National Liberal Club, where there was a very good turn out and much enthusiasm. Dear old Lincolnshire, who was 82 yesterday, made a resonant speech of the robust kind, and Birrell was quite amusing.

The plot thickens round the Oxford Chancellorship,[1] and as it seems more than probable that the Tories will run a candidate—most likely the Lord Chancellor Cave—I have agreed to put in nomination, and we will have an interesting contest, though with our friends the country clergy in full blast, the result is a foregone conclusion. Sir J. Simon, with Basil Herbert as understudy, is beating up the Oxford

---

[1] The Chancellorship of Oxford was the honour it would have gratified him most to win. Few ex-Prime Ministers have been more remarkable for those qualities of mind which a University honours, and few men have loved their University more. But the Conservative graduates were determined to oppose him on party and clerical grounds. They put forward a successful conveyancer who had just been made Lord Chancellor in the Conservative Government as their candidate. "Lord Oxford," wrote Lord Birkenhead in *The Times*, "is the greatest living Oxonian. If he were a Conservative he would be elected by acclamation. To reject him because he is a Liberal is to admit partisan prejudices as narrow as they are discreditable." But in spite of this support from a Conservative leader and the refusal of the Archbishop of Canterbury himself to vote against Lord Oxford, Lord Cave was successful.

There is little doubt that Lord Oxford felt this snub administered by his beloved University more than any disappointment, save one, in his life after he ceased to be Prime Minister.

Liberals in London, and a lot of non-party men like the judges and bishops, to come to our aid. Meanwhile I must set to work on my " Free Thought " lecture, which is due next week, and which requires careful handling. I shall come on Friday and be at The Wharf all next week, except Thursday—so I hope to see you often.

All blessings.

44 BEDFORD SQUARE,

4th June, 1925.

I have just returned from my hour with the Unitarians : a highly intelligent and enthusiastic audience at the Caxton Hall, whose hungry mouths I fed with pure milk and I fear some rather tough meat. However, they seemed to swallow and digest it all, and I kept fairly clear of the quagmires which environed my path. I gave them πάντα γέλως. It will be printed in due course and you shall have a copy.

As Margot is going to-night to *The Meistersänger*, to which the wildest of wild horses would not drag me, I think of seeing *The Cherry Orchard* for the second time, with Nan[1] as my companion : I shall be able to test one's first impressions.

I have just had a noble offer from Lady Breadalbane—a widow—who proposes to give me her late husband's (he was a K.G.) Garter robes as a present. I shall jump at this, as it will save me a lot of money.

Margot and I drive to-morrow morning to The Wharf in time for lunch. I am glad and relieved to have got Free Thought off my chest.

44 BEDFORD SQUARE,

19th June, 1925.

I dined last night with the Geoffrey Howards. Kitty, who is periodically under the surgeon's knife, has come up for another slight operation : she looked extraordinarily well.

I see that Mr. Grundy has at last succeeded in finding another candidate for the Chancellorship, and we shall now have to deal with the Cave-men. Their first list is rather a sorry, scurvy lot : the only people of any distinction are Bob Cecil (of all people) and

[1] Miss Tennant.

your friend Sir C. Sherrington : *que diable fait-il dans cette galère?* They seem to be a rump of clericals and fossil Tories, but just the sort of people to appeal to the Country Clergy : so they may succeed in doing the trick.

Elizabeth came to lunch to-day on her way to Brighton : she has slept well at the Mill House and seems to be in excellent form.

We go to Waddesdon to-morrow for Sunday, but I shall be back here fairly early on Monday. I shall come to the Balliol gaudy on Friday and see you.

44 BEDFORD SQUARE,

22nd June, 1925.

It seems an age since I heard of or from you.

The Cave-men in their ancient stronghold of primæval prejudices are, I see, being reinforced by fresh accessions from the Obscurantists. Now that the orthodox and clerical tocsin has been sounded, there will, I am sure, be a grand rally to the cavern from the parsonages and clubs—with the probable if

not inevitable result of our defeat. Do you remember
Matthew Arnold's lines ?

> Charge once more, and then be dumb.
> Let the victors, when they come,
> When the forts of folly fall,
> Find thy body by the wall !

We spent Sunday in the palatial museum of Waddesdon, which contains (*inter alia*) the finest Sir Joshuas
and Gainsboroughs in the whole world. But I did
not really enjoy myself, and came back after dinner
yesterday night in solitude, in the Royce which,
piloted by Mostyn, did a record journey. I shall be
at the Balliol gaudy on Friday evening and see you
on Saturday.

THE HOUSE OF LORDS,

23rd June, 1925.

I was so glad to get your letter. You seem to be
getting much satisfaction at present out of your
progeny. I am sorry the model is so commonplace.
I see that your friend L. of Trinity has joined the
Cave-men, otherwise the list of new adherents to the
cavern to-day is for the most part a ragged and un-
distinguished lot. I was amused to see that young

David Cecil had taken up his father's challenge and come to us. I was also glad to see the name of Bishop Gore. But unfortunately it is not the elect who form the big battalions of voters.

I am listening off and on to a dreary debate here on Agricultural Wages.

I want very much to show you my beautiful clothes : you must really come up soon and see them.

All blessings.

44 BEDFORD SQUARE,

30th June, 1925.

I have only time to scribble a line before post, as I have been kept at a long sitting at a House of Lords Committee.

The weather is perfect and we are going to dine to-night at Coombe with Juliet Trevor [1]—nearly a half-hour's drive into the country.

I was occupied yesterday with my budget speech in the House of Lords, with which I was fairly well satis-

[1] Lady Juliet Duff.

138

fied, but it is an impossible audience : as Lowe said fifty years ago, it is like " speaking by torchlight to corpses in a charnel-house." I met Winston in the street to-day, looking very summery and gay, and I think glad to have seen and heard the last of his budget. I hope to get away to The Wharf on Friday.

44 BEDFORD SQUARE,

10th July, 1925.

I have not the faintest idea what a " sweet loose " may be. One is always having to learn new vocabularies ; but as it evidently means something that marks progress in your new art I join Mrs. Phillips in her congratulations.

I had a terrific day yesterday at Mill Hill—1 to 6 : a huge and protracted luncheon with a series of boring speeches—one from Wells of Wadham in the character of Vice-Chancellor of Oxford University. Then an exhibition of the boys' athletic prowess : and finally a distribution of prizes and a brief " address " from myself, which is not badly summarised in to-day's *Daily Telegraph*. I dined with Oc and Betty, and went on with them and a couple of nice young people, male and female, to Olympia where, for the best part of three hours, we watched the Cossacks. It is a series of marvellous and almost miraculous feats of horsemanship, interspersed with songs and dances from a Russian choir : much too long and repetitive, but well worth seeing if you are content with almost an hour and a half. I got home rather tired with my day's experience.

I go to-night to the annual dinner of the Elder Brethren, in my best clothes *plus* the Garter. A pity that you can't paint me so—especially as I have had my hair cut. I hope you are able to come to dinner.

44 BEDFORD SQUARE,

14th July, 1925.

I have got places for us at *The Duck* [1] on Thursday evening. We shall have to dine about 7.15. Let me know what time to expect you. I loved our game at chess in the semi-darkness, and did not resent my deserved defeat.

I have just come back from a rather interesting lunch given by Colonel House the American—all men. Among them were Lords Reading and Grey,

[1] Ibsen's *Wild Duck*.

and the always delightful Paderewski. I sat between him and an " eminent American Senator," Walsh by name, little known here, but a great man in his own country.

I am going to-night to preside over the dinner to Mrs. Strong, where there will be a rare collection of the highest of brows, both male and female. The proceedings ought to be conducted in Latin. She is to be presented with an address in that language from the accomplished pen of Mackail.

44 Bedford Square,

24th July, 1925.

Thank you so much for your letter. I had a terrific day yesterday—six hours or thereabouts in the train going to South Wales and returning, with a sweltering afternoon meeting of about 3,000 people, to whom I discoursed on the austere topic of coal. They were a wonderful audience, understanding and taking every point, and there was quite a demonstration of enthusiasm at the station when I left.

We have just disposed of the Queen of Rumania, who came to lunch, where we had Ll. G., Desmond,

Viola and others. She is quite clever and talked amusingly, and has been in her day a great charmer.

I will come to see you at the Foundry on Sunday.

44 BEDFORD SQUARE,

30th July, 1925

I had a severe day here yesterday. Left here in the car with Violet about 4.30 for Cambridge : dined with her at the Bull and then went on to the opening of the Summer School. It was quite a good show, and I gave them a discourse mainly on the past, which was well received. The surprise was the speech of *Lady* Buckmaster, who moved the vote of thanks : quite excellent both in form and delivery. Violet stayed on for a couple of days and I drove back alone in the midnight in much comfort : I did the return journey to Bedford Square in little more than an hour and a half.

The Greats List came out this morning, and, alas, Puff only got a Second. He quite expected it, and I was more disappointed than surprised. Margot has gone off to Mells to consecrate some bells, but P. and I lunched together and made the best of the situation.

We were both in quite good spirits, and I have never known, or shall ever know, a more perfect character than his.

We had a long conclave about Land at Abingdon Street this morning : not unsatisfactory. I go to The Wharf to-morrow.

44 BEDFORD SQUARE,

3rd November, 1925.

It was a great joy to be with you on Sunday. " To-morrow and to-morrow and to-morrow creeps in this petty pace ! " But you must come up before long and see *The Gull* [1] and look round. I see the Goupil has reopened with some 500 works of art : so—for the time—even in our poor Marchant's ashes live his wonted fires. I have not been there yet, but will look in as soon as I can.

I am just going off with Margot to the Coliseum matinée to see ¼ of an hour of Lopokova in *Petrouska*.

I read in bed some of Stevenson's *New Arabian Nights*, which I had not looked at for years. They

[1] Chekov's *Seagull*.

wear fairly well, and he has left no exact successor ; but there is no doubt that one is conscious all the time of a machine very skilfully and deftly worked. The really great story-tellers are more spontaneous and less laboured.

I have been plodding away in a jog-trot fashion at the book, which has now taken me off and on the best part of ten months.

I go to Huddersfield after lunch on Thursday, and after an exacting day on Friday hope to be back here Saturday. No Wharf this week-end.

44 BEDFORD SQUARE,

10th November, 1925.

I was so glad to hear from you again after a long silence. We went this morning to St. Margaret's to the memorial service for Frances Charteris, which was very simple and moving. I think the enclosed old English prayer which they sang strikes the right note for such a character and life as hers. There was a good little sketch of her in *The Times* to-day by Cys, who was devoted to her, signed " C. A."

We have had at lunch the Dean of St. Paul's and his wife. He is a strange, isolated figure, with all the culture in the world, and a curiously developed gift of expression, but with kinks and twists, both intellectual and temperamental, which make him too freakish to be a real power. But he is the only ecclesiastic in these days who is really interesting.

I am afraid your landscaping has been cut short by this most depressing snap of shrivelling weather. I went to the Goupil yesterday, and talked to the second-in-command, who has always deputised for our poor friend Marchant. For the moment things are in the melting-pot, but he seems to think business will be reconstructed on the old lines. There were a few good pictures : a characteristic Pryde, and a charming small landscape by W. Nicholson ; and best of all an early Orpen of Dublin Bay. The two Spencers were represented, but neither of them at his best.

To-morrow is Armistice Day and I have to go to the Whitehall ceremony, which threatens rapidly to become a convention.

The Wharf is still shut up, but next week I have to go to a meeting at Newbury (Wednesday) and shall come to see you on Thursday. What are you reading ?

Blessings and all love.

44 BEDFORD SQUARE,

23rd November, 1925.

Thank you for your card. You seem to be developing a sub-career as a scene painter. The wood in *Dear Brutus* sounds a quite ambitious adventure. Is it all for love of Mr. Fagan?

The poor Queen's death[1] has upset most of the social arrangements. We are going to have the usual *éloges* in both Houses this afternoon and I am going to try to say something about her. She was the one Royalty I really loved, and her sweetness to me at all times is a memory I treasure. Happily there is going to be the minimum of fuss and display over her funeral.

I went yesterday (Sunday) afternoon, for the first time for years, to the service at Westminster Abbey. Their latest Canon, one Donaldson, preached. He was appointed by Ramsay MacDonald, and is an advanced Christian Socialist with a strong dash of High Church. In our time he once led a march of the Unemployed from Leicester to London. There were some things in his sermon which would have found an echo in your mutinous and resilient bosom, but, though fluent and at times forcible, he was not very

[1] Queen Alexandra.

impressive. It is interesting to hear this gospel preached from the pulpit of the Abbey, but he finished up with an elaborate panegyric on Queen Alexandra.

I am dipping into a rather learned book published by the Clarendon Press on the Poet Laureates, out of which I shall get a little padding for one of my last chapters.

44 Bedford Square,

29th November, 1925.

I was not able to write yesterday as a lot of people—mostly political—came and took up my time.

The funeral at Westminster Abbey on Friday was simple and dignified.[1] The snow on the ground and the absence of big crowds and noise made it more impressive. The most moving moment was when, in the absolute silence of the Abbey, where we were all sitting for the arrival of the procession, one heard in the dim distance the faint sounds of the military bands playing their dead marches as the coffin passed them. The actual ceremony was mercifully short and there was nothing histrionic about it. There is no Royalty in Europe whose death will arouse so much genuine feeling.

[1] Queen Alexandra's funeral.

147

We went in the evening yesterday to see a lately produced play by Cicely Hamilton called *The Old Adam.* It is totally without the love motive or any " triangular " situations.   Quite an original idea : two neighbouring nations having declared war finding all their armies, navies, air forces, etc., completely paralysed and motionless, through the discovery and application of a " negative ray." It is marvellously well written and almost perfectly acted by the Birmingham Repertory Company. I think you must see it, and I am quite ready to see it again. I look forward to having you here both Thursday and Friday.   The cold is cruel, and I hope you are careful not to let it get possession of you.

44 BEDFORD SQUARE,

1st December, 1925.

I am glad that you got through your drawing of " Harvard's most brilliant Poet " without being altogether *éblouie.*

Please ask Fagan for his box on Thursday.   We will wait to decide about Friday night until you come. The choice lies between *The Seagull*, *Old Adam*, and

148

The Doll's House. I have rarely known London so well supplied with good plays well acted. D'Ab [1]— who was here just now to lunch, after taking part in a ceremonial signature of the Locarno Pact at the Foreign Office, where, he says, Briand made much the best speech—reports that in Berlin seventy per cent. of the plays are English and French, and mostly English. Bernard Shaw has there an inexhaustible vogue : he was made for the Germans.

Did you read Walkley's critique to-day on *Madras House* which was reproduced last night ? " *Tous les genres sont bons hormis le genre ennuyeux ?* "—as I think Voltaire said. Write to-morrow and tell me exactly your scheme of life.

44 BEDFORD SQUARE,

9th December, 1925.

I was delighted to get your letter to-day on my return from Liverpool. I had a good tho' hurried time there. I stayed at Greenbank, the ancestral home of the once Quaker and now Unitarian Rathbones, which was built at the time of the French

---

[1] Lord D'Abernon.

Revolution. We had a choice assortment of Liverpudlian worthies both at dinner and at supper. They are quite a distinctive type, which would be more attractive if it were less flagrantly respectable. We had a very fine meeting at the Philharmonic Hall, which is the best place for such a purpose in the country. The Liverpudlians are too well bred to make a very enthusiastic audience, but they are intelligent and receptive. I had to leave early this morning to get back for the reopening of the Liberal Fair at the Albert Hall, in which ceremony Dame Margaret Ll. G. and I sang a dulcet duet in perfect tune.

Meanwhile an agreement has been patched up over the Land Policy and the Party is less agitated and tremulous—for the moment.

Alas, I shall not be with you this Sunday !

44 Bedford Square,

11th December, 1925.

I hope you find Adams a remunerative model. I think I must send you from Winsor and Newton a small keg of woad.

I have just come back from a huge public luncheon to inaugurate Arbuthnot Lane's new Health Society. I delivered a brief allocution, in which I had a dig or two at the doctors. Philip Snowden also spoke. The Dean of St. Paul's was of the company. It is quite a well-conceived movement (which finds little favour with the orthodox pundits of the profession) and may, I think, do good. Snowden told a pathetic story of a little girl at one of the London Hospitals, who, being given a glass of milk, asked wistfully, " May I drink to the bottom ? "

The Party perturbations are apparently subsiding.

Lucy writes to me that she has suddenly become interested in Hannah More, and I am sending her for a Christmas present a nice little edition, which has just come out, of H. M.'s letters. I wish I were coming to you to-morrow. We shall settle down at The Wharf at the end of this next week.

44 BEDFORD SQUARE,

18th December, 1925.

We leave here after lunch to-morrow (Saturday) for The Wharf, where we shall be off and on, and mostly on, till February.

I had a terrific day yesterday, which from first to last involved making four speeches. The presentation of E. Grey's portrait by Orpen was quite a nice function. It is not really a first-rate work of art, but of course it has merits, and gives the impression of a powerful and individual model. I finished up with a Free Trade speech in the House of Lords—the worst audience in the world : great politeness (except when " Chuck it Smith " takes the floor), but no resilience, or even response, either from friends or foes. There is no debating, and I shall only go when I have something to say that I want reported.

Our meeting of party men of " substance " in the afternoon was not bad, but not highly encouraging, and was adjourned till February.

I have been cleaning up here this morning, but my paper on " Christianity and Government " hangs fire. I have just been to see a one-act children's play at Cressida's school : she had the best part and acted quite well.

The enclosed is locally interesting. The original is, I believe, in the Abingdon Town Hall, and must be one of the oldest English pictures.

I shall see you, I trust, Sunday.

44 BEDFORD SQUARE,

27th January, 1926.

Thank you so much for your Liverpool letters. You seem to be having a pretty hectic time in your native air with the Dominie [1] for a climax.

We had a very good meeting at Hull, and I enjoyed my quiet Sunday at Castle Howard, which, however, in winter is like a vast ice house, dimly lit up here and there by oil lamps, but there is a lot of interest in the books and pictures.

When I got back here I found Antoine had arrived : he has just left this morning by the *Olympic* for New York to put in his letters of recall. He has been vilely treated. His plans for the future are of course uncertain, but happily the present Rumanian Government seems to be on its last legs. Antoine himself is in very good form and explained to Miss Campbell that no Englishman really understood the meaning of Love.

I hope to get to The Wharf on Friday evening and see you Saturday.

[1] Dr. John Sampson.

153

44 BEDFORD SQUARE,

1st February, 1926.

It was tantalising to have only such a brief glimpse of you yesterday, but we had quite amusing Bridge, and after you left I played another rubber with Arthur Lowther as partner, which almost impoverished Sir Reginald and Christopher. Didn't you think the old fellow a marvellous survival of Victorian vitality and *joie de vivre*? I doubt whether any of these degenerate Georgians will ever live to see their 79th birthday, and if they do it will be only as " lean and slipper'd pantaloons."

I drove back this morning into the whirlpool here, which is seething with petty currents and eddies. The usual dinners on the night before Parliament meets are being given this evening, and I shall go to the one which Beauchamp provides for the Liberal Peers. After it, Lady B. is giving a reception for the Liberal ladies, which I fear for the first time will not be graced by the presence and pearls of Lady M.

Puffin writes enthusiastically about the good time which he and Elizabeth are having in the centre of the Film World. They are guests of Douglas Fairbanks and Mary Pickford : Charlie Chaplin drops

in to meals : Lilian Gish hovers about in the offing :
and (to Puffin the climax) he has had ten minutes
with Pauline Frederick. *Que voulez-vous ?*

44 BEDFORD SQUARE,

5th February, 1926.

I hope you got the little parcel of books I sent you
yesterday. I threw in amongst the thrills a serious
little monograph on Darwin—which is not very good
but quite instructive. I forget whether you have our
new friend *David* Somerville's *Gladstone and Disraeli* ?
If not I will send it you. She (i.e. David's wife) sent
me as a present for myself a packet of raisins and
almonds : which was very thoughtful of her. It
reminded me of Wordsworth's lines about the best
part of a good man's life—"His little nameless
unremember'd acts of kindness and of love."

I am going this evening to see *The Ghost Train*,
under the chaperonage of Mrs. Heneage. I hope to
get one or two good thrills, but am not very sanguine.

I have just finished the two-page Preface to my book
and have only now to compose an equally brief
Epilogue. It has been a great resource to me this
last year : especially during my time in Egypt.

I must now start on my *Reminiscences*, or whatever they are to be called—I am glad of a definite task. The notion that as you grow old you need rest and nothing to do is the purest moonshine.

44 BEDFORD SQUARE,

7th February, 1926.

The Ghost Train is quite worth seeing, for its novel " effects " and good melodramatic surprises. It has no literary merits. I don't feel inclined to go and see Ainley and Madge in Benedick and Beatrice. Do you remember how tired we got once at Stratford of Dogberry and his clownish team, and still more of the silly episode of Hero ?

I went yesterday afternoon with some children—two little Lambtons ; Cressida and Laura as usual had " colds "—to see a film—*Rin-Tin-Tin*—one of a series of which an Alsatian hound is the hero. This time he played the part of a wolf, caught as a puppy and more or less tamed. It was most exciting. The scene being snowfields somewhere at the back of Canada, with a " shack " and a gold mine, a half-breed villain, sleighs drawn by teams of noble-looking dogs, etc., etc. " Rin-Tin " behaved with infinite resource and fidelity under the most trying conditions, his eyes flowing with tears over the body of his dead master ; and after countless fights and escapes ending up by rocking the cradle of two bottle-fed twins in the shack, with a litter of his own family of wolf cubs in the next room. It is the kind of film I infinitely prefer to the ordinary American sob-stuff.

Eliz. and Puffin are still with the Fairbanks, and he is making a serious study of the technique.

We are in a fog here : I hope you are better off.

44 BEDFORD SQUARE,

12th February, 1926.

We are still in Cimmerian darkness here with almost constant rain, which makes it impossible to go outside with any pleasure or profit.

I am beginning to collect materials for my new book, and all the odds and ends that I have in drawers or which recur to my memory are entombed for the time being in a huge envelope.

We have just had a lunch here at which the guests were Sir J. and Lady Forbes-Robertson, Haselden (who does the caricature sketches) and his wife, and

Desmond MacCarthy. Sir J. is a splendid old boy, originally by profession a painter, and certainly the best Shakespearian actor we have had in my time. He is still full of life and interests. His daughter has a good part in *Vanya*, and we will all go there together, if, as I hope, you will come on Thursday evening. We dined with Ethel Sands to-night in Chelsea.

Do you see the reviews of Walter Raleigh's letters just published in two vols. ? There is sure to be good stuff in them, and I loved him as a companion. But it must be admitted that he could both write and talk (when he was in the mood) greater nonsense than almost any really clever man I have known.

44 BEDFORD SQUARE,

4th March, 1926.

I was delighted to see your handwriting this morning. I quite agree about your little visit last week. Olga's was a *cri de cœur*.[1] I have found out now that the actress who played the part, under the *nom de théâtre* Mary Sheridan, is really the young Graham girl who married Kenneth Barnes some weeks ago. I think she has real promise, don't you ?

[1] Chekov's *Three Sisters.*

Yesterday afternoon I took the chair at King's College at a lecture by Ramsay Muir on Gladstone : one of a series they have been having on English Prime Ministers. It was quite first rate, both in matter and form, and there was a crowded audience, male and female, of 700 or 800, with High, Middle and Low Brows.

I have finished Beatrice Webb's *Apprenticeship*—a remarkable story in its way. To me hers is, *au fond*, a tiresome type of mind, but she has lived, ever since she was eighteen, an independent and industrious and at times adventurous life. And it is to the credit both of her insight and character that, being lapped in bourgeois luxury, and really very good-looking, she finally at the age of thirty married Sidney Webb, a highly-knowledgable *Saint*. Since then in their partnership they have jointly produced some twenty solid, though for the most part unreadable, books.

All love.

44 BEDFORD SQUARE,

12th March, 1926.

I wish you had been with me at Gilbert Murray's lecture on " The Personality of Gibbon." It was quite first rate both in substance and form, with ironic and humorous asides, and beautifully delivered.

Yesterday afternoon we took the two little Bonnie-Carters, Cressida and Laura, to the new Douglas Fairbanks film *The Black Pirate*. It is coloured and on the whole with success. It is full of thrilling moments and hair-breadth adventures, and the great Douglas's acrobatic feats in climbing ships' sides and slitting sails, and diving and swimming a sea as transparent as the water of an aquarium with about fifty others, are quite beyond belief. The other thing which I want to see is *The Sea Beast*—a filming of *Moby Dick*, with John Barrymore as Captain Ahab.

We dined last night at Winston's in Downing Street, where Clemmie [1] boasted that she had collected for my special benefit a " Corps de Ballet " ; and there certainly were some well-favoured specimens of your sex and of the other. F. E. (rather wasted by his bad illness), Horne, Douglas Hogg, and other minor political lights. It was quite interesting.

We come to The Wharf to-morrow and I shall drive over to you on Sunday morning.

[1] Mrs. Winston Churchill.

44 BEDFORD SQUARE,

16th March, 1926.

It was a great joy to see you on Sunday. Your entourage was singularly variegated : almost a satire on rural solitude. Anything less bucolic in composition can hardly be conceived. Your stories of this hectic and depraved Bloomsbury, in which I live my homely, virtuous days and nights, still linger in my memory.

I saw some wonderful horses at Whatcombe—a pleasure to look upon.

We have had a nice German couple here to lunch to-day : Dr. and Mrs. Simon, who are returning to work in their Foreign Office in Berlin. I get more and more out of conceit with the Latin races.

I have been reading in bed an excellent book which I must send you : *Sanders,* by the detective writer Edgar Wallace, but quite a new departure for him, as the scene is laid among African tribes, and the hero a British " Commissioner "—as they ought to be, but rarely are.

I have a rather tiresome week before me : its duties include " laying a stone " for the new buildings of *The Daily News* on Thursday : going that evening by the midnight train to Glasgow ; attending on Friday evening a banquet there in honour of Sir Daniel Stevenson : and proceeding on Saturday morning to Edinburgh to deliver to the Classical Association an address on " Scaliger," still not half finished and requiring some research.

Write to me.

44 BEDFORD SQUARE,

18th March, 1926.

I have been very busy putting the finishing touches to my " Scaliger," which has cost me a certain amount of research and is due for delivery at Edinburgh at 3 p.m. on Saturday. It contains (amongst other unreadable matter) a lot of Latin and one or two Greek quotations. An excellent young woman came here yesterday morning to type it, and I have now three beautiful " typescripts " to take with me in case of accidents.

I am going to present the " Hawthornden " prize (£100) for the best thing of the year next Tuesday afternoon at the Aeolian Hall to O'Casey for his

Paycock. Margot has met him at lunch, and says he is delightful.

At Grillion's last night I sat between G. Dawson (Editor of *The Times*) and O. Seaman (Editor of *Punch*), both new members.

To-day I helped with T. P. to lay two foundation stones for the new buildings of *The Daily News* and *Star*. We had quite an amusing lunch afterwards, at which all big-wigs of the London Press were present, and T. P. and I discoursed to them.

I am off to Glasgow at midnight for a function in honour of old Sir D. Stevenson. I shall be back here for breakfast on Monday.

44 BEDFORD SQUARE,

22nd March, 1926.

I had rather a strenuous time in Scotland. I left here by the midnight train on Thursday and spent Friday in Glasgow, where I spoke in the evening at the Stevenson dinner. On Saturday morning I motored to Edinburgh, not an interesting drive till you are close to your destination. The distant view of Edinburgh in the sun and haze is one of the most beautiful in Europe. I gave my lecture in the afternoon to the Classical pundits : stiff stuff even for them ; there is a good report of the larger half of it in *The Times* to-day. Then I dined with them in the evening. I stayed the night in a comfortable house, where I have several times put up, with a most friendly couple, Sir Robert and Lady Maule. I accompanied them to the Kirk on Sunday morning, heard an excellent sermon, and witnessed the quaint ceremony of the " Induction " of an Elder. I returned to London after dinner by the night train.

To-morrow afternoon I am going to a little affair at the Aeolian Hall, to present the annual prize for the best work of imagination of the year to Sean O'Casey for his *Paycock*. On Wednesday we have our debate in the House of Lords on the Geneva muddle.

I hope to come to The Wharf on Friday for the week-end. Could you come to dinner Sunday night ? Elizabeth and Puffin ought to be with us by then.

44 BEDFORD SQUARE,

23rd March, 1926.

The poor little Bonnie-Carters, except Cressida, who is still immune, are all laid low with the measles. It spoils their Easter, and of course they cannot come to The Wharf.

Phyllis Boyd and her French husband [1] came here to lunch to-day. I had not seen him before : he seems quite a nice type of Anglo-Frenchman. Phyllis is always delightful. Venetia, who has been three months in India, also turned up.

We went after lunch to the Aeolian Hall and I there gave the Hawthornden prize. I delivered a short allocution. Old Lady Gregory, who is the grand-mother of the Abbey Theatre, gave a discourse—quite good : and told me all the details of O'Casey's youth and career. He made a reply, which began in Irish and ended in English, which was modest and in good taste. He is a strange-looking, rather tousled, Dublin man, and I liked him. There was quite a good gathering of the " intellectuals " of London (Gosse, etc.) : and it was a pleasant little ceremony.

The Geneva fiasco [2] is being debated in the Commons, and to-morrow in the Lords. I shall try to point the various morals. My Edinburgh lecture has been well reported.

Blessings.

[1] The Comte de Jansi.

[2] This is a reference to the failure of the Conference at Geneva to ratify the Pact of Locarno. It was part of the Locarno agreement that Germany should enter the League of Nations, and Germany had made it clear that her application to join the League was dependent upon her receiving a permanent seat on the Council of the League. At the Geneva Conference seats were given to Poland, Spain and Brazil.

165

44 Bedford Square,

20th April, 1926.

I came up here this morning : mainly to have an interview with the Cardinal,[1] whom I have just left. He was in the main sensible and reasonable and will use his authority to prevent any change. I did not care for him, but the princes of the Church have no message for me.

We are going—a family party—to see Marie Tempest in *Cat's Cradle* this evening.

I have had (in response to gifts of " Scaliger ") a nice letter from Baldwin, and two quite interesting ones from the Bishop of Oxford and Dean Inge of St. Paul's. The last mentioned (to illustrate what education was in the time of Henry VIII and Queen Elizabeth) quoted from a treatise of 1530 the author's recommendation that a child should begin Greek at seven, and " in the meantime " use Latin as a " familiar language." Aristophanes, Homer, Virgil, Ovid, etc. " will suffice until he pass the age of *thirteen* years." No wonder that Lady Jane Grey (at sixteen)

---

[1] Cardinal Bourne. The subject of the interview was the question of the education of Lord Oxford's grandson, the present Lord Oxford, whose mother had joined the Church of Rome.

was conversant with Hebrew, and that Mary Queen of Scots wrote excellent Latin verses, and that Queen Elizabeth could talk with the foreign Ambassadors in at least four different languages. What a falling off we show !

I shall come back to-morrow afternoon to The Wharf.

44 BEDFORD SQUARE,

28th April, 1926.

We went to Stanway on Monday evening to see the Play [1] again. The children actors were quite perfect. The audience this time included Goonie Churchill and Diana Duff Cooper. I would gladly see it again, but they are all growing, and can never be recaptured.

I came up yesterday morning and met my little Conclave at Abingdon Street : Ll. G. etc., etc. In the evening we went, almost as a family, to the Haymarket, and saw the ridiculously-named *That Woman Business*, from which I expected little. It is light stuff

---

[1] A play written for the grandchildren of Lord and Lady Wemyss, and performed by them at Stanway.

with good dialogue, and a quite novel set of situations, and one of the best casts you can imagine. Every part was well done, there was no sentiment false or otherwise, and you could laugh the whole time with an untroubled conscience. You must see it when you come here.

I am just off to the " Charnel House " to hear Buckmaster on Birth Control. It is a vile day, which began with a black fog and has now melted into a dreary drizzle. Our Windsor week-end is off ; so I shall see you on Sunday after speaking at Watford on Friday night.

Blessings and love.

44 BEDFORD SQUARE,

4th May, 1926.

We are plunged into the cataract of the Strike,[1] and already London presents an abnormal aspect. I have not been out yet to-day, but I am going to start very soon for the H. of L., where we shall have some sort of a debate about the Coal situation. I cannot think that the General Strike will last long :

[1] The General Strike.

it is very unpopular and they are short of funds for anything like a severe struggle. We have very few newspapers to-day, and to-morrow it is said that we shall have none. Even *The Times*, which is printed by non-Union men, cannot get itself circulated and distributed. Puffin, who has enlisted with his little car to help with supplies, was out practically the whole night. He and his friends who are too young to have been in the war are quite enjoying the sense of adventure, with irregular hours and strange errands.

I went for half-an-hour yesterday afternoon to the Academy, which is a poverty-stricken spectacle. I have never seen such a lot of incredibly bad portraits, and Orpen is almost the worst offender. The Nigger and Nude picture ought not to have been hung, not because it is nasty (I have seen many a nastier), but because it is badly drawn and painted, and has no kind of distinction. I agree with *The Sunday Times* man that Mrs. Procter's " Back Bedroom " and H. Knight's " Girl reading a Bible " are the two best things there. Both are on quite a small scale, and Knight's is like a good Dutch painting.

I have got to make two speeches—on very different themes : so I must stop. As most locomotion is for the moment at a standstill, I hope I may get to The Wharf on Friday.

44 BEDFORD SQUARE,

6th May, 1926.

We are still in the throes of the General Strike and all our young people are hard at work in keeping things going. Katherine Tennant, who has just been here at lunch, takes out her car every morning at about seven, and fetches shop girls, typists, etc., from the East End to their work in the city. Puffin plies his little car in north London and brings out-patients to and from the hospitals : later in the day he picks up stray people who are stranded in the streets, and takes them to their homes in the suburbs. The papers are beginning to reappear, and this morning we have an attenuated copy of *The Times.* The trains are running better—what with men dribbling back to their work and a horde of volunteer workers. It is much easier to supply vacancies than it would have been in pre-war times before people had become accustomed to be commandeered. The whole thing is a piece of criminal folly, which will soon break to pieces.

I have just finished an article for my American magazine on Dictatorships.

44 BEDFORD SQUARE,

11th May, 1926.

I loved being with you on Sunday, and exploring together the avenues which we have trodden all these years.

When I came up yesterday morning to our "Shadow Cabinet" at Abingdon Street, there was one notable absentee—Ll. G.—who was in the sulks, and had cast in his lot for the moment with the clericals—Archbishops and Deans and the whole company of the various Churches (a hopeless lot)—in the hope of getting a foot-hold for himself in the Labour camp. He is already, being a creature of uncertain temperature, suffering from cold feet. So much so, that I have a message this morning from Miss Stevenson asking me to arrange for a joint meeting in July at Carnarvon, which he and I are to address !

The streets here to-day are full of symptoms of return to normal life : buses and tubes running, and more volunteers, male and female, than there are places to fill. E. Grey came to lunch in excellent form : and we are having to dinner to-day A. J. Balfour and Birrell and Desmond MacCarthy.

171

Margot and I went after lunch to Lefevre's Gallery in King's Street to see the Seurats, which are very interesting. He died at the age of thirty, as far back as 1891. I don't care for his *pointillism*, but one can see that he had the makings of a really great artist. I think we are approaching the revival of common sense.

44 BEDFORD SQUARE,

3rd June, 1926.

Thank you so much for your letter. As St. Paul says (1 Cor. xv.), I have been " fighting after the manner of men with beasts at Ephesus."[1] But the air

[1] The phrase " fighting with beasts at Ephesus " probably refers to the consequences of Mr. Lloyd George's conduct during the general strike in May ; his withdrawal from the party Councils, and the indications he had given by speech and in the American press that, in the event of the strike being prolonged, he was in favour of negotiation. That course had appeared to Lord Oxford equivalent to a surrender of a fundamental principle not only of Liberalism but of government. " If the leaders of the Liberal Party as a body had adopted Mr. Lloyd George's view," he wrote to the Liberal Chief Whip on June 1st, " we should have been doing our best to weaken the authority of the Government, which was for the moment the embodiment and organ of the national self-defence against the gravest domestic danger which has threatened the country in our time . . . Mr. Lloyd George," he added, " was not driven out, he refused to come in " ; and

s clearing now, and all the people I care for have
been wonderfully affectionate and loyal.

By way of distraction we went yesterday to the
Derby on the foulest day on which it had ever been
run. It poured incessantly from 2 a.m. until we left
the course. We were as sheltered and comfortable
as the elements would allow, in the excellent box of
Sir Abe Bailey, nearly opposite the winning-post.
I was wise enough to back nothing, but I saved some
of the clients who applied to me for tips by restraining
them from losing their money on such favourites as
Colorado and Swift and Sure. The crowd, draggled
and shivering under umbrellas, though large, was not
to be compared with what it was on the sweltering
summer day when I last visited the Downs to witness
the victory of Spion Kop.

Lord Oxford concluded his letter by saying, " I will not continue
to hold the leadership for a day unless I am satisfied that I retain
in full measure the confidence of the party." Liberals thus
found themselves forced to choose between two leaders. On
June 3rd (the date of this letter), the Liberal members of the
House of Commons sent Sir John Simon and Sir Godfrey
Collins, the Chief Whip, on a deputation to Lord Oxford at
Bedford Square, hoping that the difference might be bridged ;
Lord Oxford replied that his view of the issue remained un-
changed. On June 8th, the Parliamentary Liberal Party passed
a resolution deploring the publication of the differences between
their leaders. This was equivalent to a vote of censure on Lord
Oxford. But on June 11th the Liberal and Radical Candidates'
Association (after listening to a speech from Mr. Lloyd George)
appointed a deputation to represent to Lord Oxford its " strong

I was interested in your account of the Russian play. How well I can realise that now familiar atmosphere !

It is sad that you should be reduced to drawing your own hand, not at all a bad and rather an exacting model by the way. I have nothing worth recommending to read.

desire for complete unity within the party under his leadership." Sudden illness prevented him receiving that deputation, and compelled him to cancel his engagement to address a meeting of the National Liberal Federation at Weston-super-Mare.

He had kept personal feelings (though, of course, as passages of these letters have revealed, they existed) so completely apart from his conduct as a public man, that he might have reasonably expected his followers to believe him when he declared it was no longer possible to work with Mr. Lloyd George. If he had—at last—lost patience, would not Liberals believe that he had good reason to do so ? But the diminished Liberal Party hesitated to believe that differences could not again be patched up, and the majority were unwilling to choose between him and the author of the 1918 election, now presenting himself as the champion of " progressive Liberalism " as opposed to " the official gang." I think that the shock of finding that the majority of at any rate *audible* Liberals were inclined to follow the instigator of the Coupon election of 1918 in preference to himself, had not a little to do with that slight stroke which prevented him from restating his case on the public platform. Some time afterwards, while trying in conversation to date some trivial occurrence, he inadvertently used an expression which gave me a glimpse into what he had felt at that time. " Yes," he said, " that happened while I was trying to recover from my wound." Such self-revelations were very rare in his talk, and I remembered it.

44 BEDFORD SQUARE,

9th June, 1926.

I was glad to get your note. I went yesterday to the Guildhall to see Lord Reading get the freedom of the City : I was well received by the City Fathers. R. spoke much better than I have ever heard him. He came to lunch to-day with Buckmaster and our friend the ex-Midianite.[1] We had some excellent talk. After lunch I drove with D'Ab. to the Tate Gallery to the Annual Meeting of the National Arts Collection Fund—an excellent institution. We both spoke : I mainly on the new statuette of Socrates in the British Museum, and the necessity of saving Waterloo Bridge. There was quite a crowd, mainly of your sex ; and after it was over I went through two or three of the galleries with the experts. Among all the new French pictures which Courtauld has bought and presented, the one which dominated the rest was Degas' " Man "—whose name I forget—in the library, sitting at the writing-table with the bookshelves behind him : you remember it of course : one of the most impressive of portraits.[2]

The " Liberal split " is running its course to its goal not far off : a dissolution of partnership between

---

[1] Lord D'Abernon. [2] Monsieur Duranti.

Ll. G. and myself, with all my respectable and capable colleagues. It had to come, and though it is disagreeable for the moment, because of the thickheadedness of honest and devoted followers, it is as well that it should be put through now as later on. I am going to make a speech at a luncheon on Saturday.

44 BEDFORD SQUARE,

10th June, 1926.

Things have rather taken a turn to-day, and they offer me a rather profuse resolution of confidence without any reservations, which I do not see my way to refuse. It won't alter the fundamental situation, but it saves a certain amount of irritating controversy.

I have just been with Margot to see the Epsteins at the Leicester Galleries. I don't really care for him : he is neither quite grandiose, nor (but rarely) beautiful. But there is a little head of a " Seraph " which is attractive. We went on to the Chenil Gallery, where there is an exhibition of A. John and his sister. The sister's things (Gwen, she is called) are really better than his : in a beautiful low tone. Elizabeth's portrait with the mantilla is at last sold to a man in Buffalo (U.S.A.) for 1,200 guineas.

I have been a good deal worried one way and another this last week, and it is sweet to know that your " spirit is with me."

I shall see you Sunday.

44 BEDFORD SQUARE,

11*th June*, 1926.

I was delighted by your letter this morning. I am glad that you liked my little speech at the Tate. The report in the newspapers condensed it, of necessity, and I think omitted my reference to the statuette of Socrates, just added to the British Museum, which is much the most interesting new find of the last twelve months. Did you see to-day the extraordinary prices realised by the Carmichael Raeburns? 8,000 gns. etc. I saw them at Sotheby's and they are excellent of their kind, but there is something ridiculous in the pecuniary standard of artistic values. The little Socrates, which is worth ten times as much as all the Raeburns put together, was bought for £1,200.

The squalid controversy about our Party " splits " still goes on. I have too much sympathy with our honest, hardworking, ill-informed rank and file to be hasty in dispelling their visions and aspirations after "unity." But unless they are prepared to give me a whole-hearted and unreserved vote of confidence, I shall in the course of the next three days tell them (with equal unreserve) God's truth about Ll. G. As you know, it would be nothing but a relief to me to wash my hands of the whole thing.

We are going this evening to see Noel Coward's new play—*Easy Virtue*—of which I don't expect much. But I want to sample the American actress—Jane Cowl—who is queen of the stage over there.

THE WHARF,
SUTTON COURTENAY,

31st August, 1926.

I was delighted to hear from you and to know that in another week's time you will be once more within reach. I have not been so long without seeing you since I don't know when—certainly for years. I gather from what you write of your short and simple annals that your seasiding has been a success.

We have had gorgeous weather here this last week—a blazing sun all day and now and then almost a sultry atmosphere. Violet's children are still at the

Mill House. Priscilla is now settled at Westgate and seems to be doing well.

I have been steadily doing my quota of writing every day and have made some progress with my book. I have read nothing really interesting ; a few shockers and Trevelyan's *History of England*. I see that you have been driven to browse in the old familiar pastures of Rider Haggard and Anthony Hope.

Puffin is back at his film work in London—which is quite an exacting job—from 9 a.m. till nearly dinner-time, and sometimes a night séance.

Margot has begun a novel of 80,000 words ! and Elizabeth is also full of literary activity. She leaves us on Saturday to accompany Antoine to Geneva to the League of Nations.

THE MANOR HOUSE,
MELLS,
FROME,

25th September, 1926.

I got your nice little letter at Sutton Bingham. I am afraid you are feeling rather solitary without the children. Why don't you arrange with Lucy to come for this next Sunday to Easton Grey, arriving, say, on Friday? I hope to get there Thursday evening, and it would be truly delightful to have some days together. I am sure Lucy would be only too glad, and incidentally you could talk about houses with her.

I had a nice unexciting time with the Heneages, seeing something of Sir Matthew Nathan who is their neighbour, and taking drives through the lovely country. I went one day to the famous Swannery at Abbotsbury near Weymouth—a fine sight; there are 800 wild swans and cygnets, and they and their ancestors have been there for 800 years.

I came here on Friday evening: there is nobody (except Baker) but the family which includes my two eldest granddaughters. Helen, who is in good looks, goes up for her first term to Somerville on Oct. 15th. Perdita is to spend the autumn and winter in Paris with her Mother: they have been lucky in having a charming flat lent to them for nothing.

I am going to London this Wed. only for the night: to attend a conclave of the " faithful."

The weather has been lovely till to-day when it has broken. The parson here is the Irish writer who adopts the name of " George A. Birmingham " ; he is called Hannay in real life and is good company and a competent preacher.

I am here till Wednesday morning.

All blessings, beloved one,

H.

44 BEDFORD SQUARE,

13th October, 1926.

The plot thickens here and our secrets are well kept, if one may judge by the inane and inept guess-work of " organs " like *The Evening Standard,* etc.

I had a conclave of the faithful at Edward Grey's on Monday evening. They all approved the course I am taking,[1] and a wagon-load of them are coming to the meeting on Friday—including Grey himself, Simon, Runciman, etc., etc. We shall make a brave show.

I am sending you as part of the *mémoires pour servir* a copy of the confidential memorandum which I sent to my colleagues for their meeting last Monday. (Of course, keep it for yourself.) The published letter,

[1] Resignation of the Party Leadership.

which will appear in the papers on Friday morning, is not so detailed, though I think more forcible.

We leave here to-morrow at midnight for Glasgow, where after the Greenock meeting we spend the night. I shall be heartily glad when this affair is over, and I am once more relatively a free man.

GLENCONNER,
NORTH BERWICK,

17th October, 1926.

You have been a very good correspondent, and I should have written more often and fully but that (as you may imagine) I have been, as the Scripture says, " compassed about with a cloud " of people to see and things to say and do.

The meeting at Greenock [1] on Friday night was unique in my experience, at moments thrilling in its intensity. There were a lot of my old and trusty friends from Paisley there, as well as good men and true from all parts of Scotland. I have not a doubt

[1] On October 15th, at Greenock, Lord Oxford made his farewell speech as Leader of the Liberal Party.

that I have taken the only wise and honourable course, and I was sure that you would agree with me.

We came here on Saturday, and shall stay to the end of the week. It is cold, but the sun shines a good part of the day, and yesterday I re-visited our old, familiar links at Archerfield. My mother-in-law and the kleines Schwesterlein [1] are here, and Rachel MacCarthy : so we are quite at peace.

I am glad that the painting progresses, and all blessings.

44 BEDFORD SQUARE,

25th October, 1926.

I was delighted with your letter. Your working hours are closed in by the shortening days, and you are right not to spend your nights at the Foundry.

I was really sorry to leave North Berwick. We had a week of almost unclouded sun and no wind, and I greatly enjoyed my golf on the ideal course (for me) at Archerfield. I played better than I had hoped, and in a match in which Katherine and I engaged a young Scottish Tory M.P.—Skelton by name—my

---

[1] One of his two sisters-in-law, Katherine and Nancy, the daughters of Sir Charles Tennant by his second wife.

putting was almost worthy of the renowned American, Bobbie Jones. The two sisters are the nicest of girls, and we had great fun together.

I have had some wonderful letters—almost the best, which came this morning, from Baldwin. I will show it you when I come. We had to lunch to-day Mackenzie King—the Liberal Prime Minister of Canada, a very good fellow without much distinction, and Ronald Lindsay, who goes off in a day or two to succeed D'Ab. at the British Embassy at Berlin : no easy job.

I have told the Oxford people to send you two tickets for the Union function on Thursday afternoon at 3. I shall be at The Wharf for some days.

THE WHARF,
SUTTON COURTENAY,

21st November, 1926.

I was so sorry not to be able to come to you this morning, but I was snatched away in the beautiful sunshine to go to Frilford to make up a foursome at golf. Though it was rather crowded, we were able to play nine holes, which I enjoyed, as I am not playing badly, and put in two or three quite sensational long distance putts : with the result that my side was victorious. It clouded over and we had some rain before the finish.

I can't tell you how I enjoyed our evening together. It brought back some of the best of our old times, and I have never seen you look more or be more your real self.

44 BEDFORD SQUARE,

24th November, 1926.

I wish I had been with you at the Strindberg play.[1] You seem to be well supplied with a varied dramatic diet at present.

I saw the last of the Dominion " statesmen " yesterday at a luncheon given to Hertzog, who is the best looking of the lot and plausible to talk to. They don't seem to have done much good by their visit, and there is a good deal of cool assurance in Australia and New Zealand approving of the insane Singapore " base," without offering to pay a shilling towards the cost, which may very likely be some 20 millions.

Margot is off to Westgate to see Priscilla. I am going with the Schwesterlein to *Princess Ida,* which I haven't seen for thirty years.

[1] *Spook Sonata.*

44 Bedford Square,

15th December, 1926.

I confess that I felt a certain attraction to Anita Berry, though on closer acquaintance she might prove a little overwhelming.

I like Chekov's endearments ; " little whale," " little beetle," etc., etc. There is a great gulf fixed between the Slavs and ourselves, and I am not sure that it will ever be bridged.

I was nosing about at Bumpus's in a spare hour this afternoon, without much in the way of discovery : but I bought for 15*s.* a Life of Mrs. Hemans, in 2 volumes, which, if it fulfils my expectations or hopes, I will make over to you.

I did not, of course, go to the Grey dinner on Monday, but I gather that it was a great success. He certainly told some home truths, but I am not sure that in expression they were sufficiently poignant and compelling to arrest our weaklings who are going a-whoring after Ll. G.

I went this morning to poor Lord Emmott's funeral service at a hideous South Kensington church, in Ennismore Gardens. It is only a week to-morrow since he was at my dinner and I had a talk with him. He was at least seven years younger than I am, and in the full vigour of his sound and unimaginative, but beneficent and unselfish Lancashire nature. He died without any premonition or pain. May my end when it comes be the same !

44 BEDFORD SQUARE,

20th January, 1927.

I should have written before, but that I have been driven about from pillar to post. I am trying to foresee the things (books, etc.) which I shall need in the sunny south to carry on my writing. One always leaves something quite indispensable behind.

We went on Monday night *en famille* with Desmond to see *Broadway*, quite the most unique presentation of the latest phases of the New York under-world : at least a half or two-thirds of the dialogue is as unintelligible to English ears as if it was Yiddish or Slovak. But I have never seen better stage management or *décor*, and as there are two murders on the stage, one by a gunman and the other by a gunwoman, and a very sleek, imperturbable detective, popping in and out at unexpected moments, there is a plentiful supply of thrills.

I also went with Margot to the Flemish Exhibition at the Academy. It is a really marvellous and most impressive collection—abundance of the best Van Dycks and Rubens, and, what is far more interesting, a wonderful array of Primitives—Van Eycks, etc., and (later) Memling. You should certainly come up one day to see them : it is at present terribly crowded, but it goes on until well into March.

Your neighbour Mr. Priestley has kindly sent me his new novel—*Adam in Moonshine*. I haven't yet finished it, but it interests and amuses me a lot. It is an almost extravagant fantasy, and (I think) rather suffers from being over-written, but well worth reading.

SPRINGLANDS,
CANNES,

31st January, 1927.

In this lavishly equipped house all the notepaper and envelopes are of abnormal tints and shapes. I have chosen one of the more modest type.

Until to-day, when we are having the unwonted experience of a thunderstorm with pouring rain, the weather has been divine : unbroken sunshine and no wind, and we have seen all the surrounding country under the best conditions. The old villages in almost inaccessible crannies on the tops of the hills are quite untouched and most picturesque. The actual Riviera is vulgarised and villa-ridden and terribly overbuilt ; but here we have a beautiful big garden, which hides everything from view, except the sea and the Esterel mountains.

I keep aloof (as it is easy to do) from the madding crowd, which gambles and races and plays tennis. We have a most considerate hostess who lets us do exactly what we like, and a house party of nice and unexciting guests : amongst them Sir Gilbert Parker the novelist, Frank Lascelles, a pageant producer, who lives in a manor house near Banbury, a Miss Holman, who is a vocalist of some facility and given up to good works, and a delightful French family of an old Protestant stock—the father a painter, with an attractive wife and daughter (Simone aged 21). They are all at intervals rehearsing a play which is to be produced at the end of the week. There are no books to speak of in the house, and I have been reading old friends, Izaak Walton's *Lives*, and Walter Raleigh's little book on Shakespeare, which is quite excellent : sane and vivid and not hysterical. We go on next Sunday to Lou Sueil, Eze. Write and tell me everything.

Lou Sueil,

Eze,

8th February, 1927.

I was sad at your catalogue of worries and troubles. I do hope that Anne is making her way out of the wood: happily it [1] is not now nearly such a formidable disease as it used to be in the days of my youth.

The weather has broken here, and for the last two days we have had a full measure of that infernal scourge—the mistral. When it does come it has to blow itself out, which takes some time. This is one of the newly-created beauty spots of Europe. We are 1,200 feet above the sea, with Monaco at our feet and a magnificent view of headlands and mountains. The little village of Eze, perched on the top of a rock, with its old houses and castle huddled up together, is as picturesque as anything in Provence. This house has been built on the next pinnacle and does infinite credit to the architect : it is in the best romanesque of the Provençal type with round arches and pillars with capitals. Our hostess, the ex-Duchess, is an attractive creature and is for the first time in her life really happy. Her husband, who is in business in a

[1] Scarlet fever.

large way, is an agreeable and well-mannered French-
man who adores her.

We have two or three English fellow-guests, including Winston Churchill's wife and the widow Ribblesdale. Until the weather broke we played golf every
day on one of the quaintest courses in Europe—Mont
Agel—3,000 feet high, with ups and downs fitted for
chamois. The view is superb, and with the aid of a
hefty female caddie I surmounted the obstacles with
success.

I have come across very few books worth mentioning.
I have been sent a new novel—*Adam's Breed*—by a
woman, which seems perfectly fresh, and so far as I
have gone, really good both in character and style.
Let me hear from you.

All love and blessings.

44 BEDFORD SQUARE,

28th February, 1927.

This brings you all my love for your birthday and
the whole year.

Stanley Spencer seems at last to have found favour
with the critics : nothing could be more appreciative

in intention—though crude and clumsy in expression —than to-day's article in *The Times*.

I looked in again passing the Goupil, and confirmed my first impressions. I see *The Times'* man says that the Cookham "Resurrection" ought to be bought for the nation.

Margot returned from Paris on Saturday afternoon in time for Elizabeth's birthday celebrations—the star of the occasion was Puffin's idol, Miss Pauline Frederick, of Film fame, who is going to appear this week on the Lyceum stage in a " straight " play. She sat next to me at dinner and I found her quite intelligent and attractive. She is of an older generation than the Gishes and has been on the boards ever since she was a child. Like all the professionals, she has only one topic. After dinner there were a few " stunts," the best being by Sarah Allgood, who sang some charming Irish songs, and Nelson Keys, who gave some life-like imitations of Gerald du Maurier and Henry Ainley.

BEDFORD SQUARE,

6th March, 1927.

I was so glad to get your letter. I agree as regards the *Nymph*, the book is better than the play. The actress whom I liked the most—little Helen Spencer who did Tessa's sister—you don't mention. I did not think Elissa Landi good as Antonia. Poor Cathleen Nisbett bemoans her part : it is an impossible one. We went to the after-show at the 200th night, and I had a nice little talk with Edna Best.

Margot went again to see " The Resurrection " and foregathered with Stanley Spencer, with whom she was so much taken that she asked him to dinner, notwithstanding his plea that he had no dress suit. So he came on Friday to a little party, which included Lord Haldane and his sister Elizabeth, with whom I talked about her *George Eliot*. Everybody, including our Elizabeth, was delighted with Stanley, who talked well and was companionable.

Margot got a chill and has been and still is in bed—though on the way to recovery. She has been reading in her seclusion the book which for the moment intrigues everybody—*Jew Süss*. It does not sound very alluring, but I am going to attack it.

I am writing away at my book and wish sometimes I had more clay to my straw. Winston's seems to be a curious compound of fine writing and boisterous clap-trap. Write to me.

44 BEDFORD SQUARE,

25th March, 1927.

I have been busy in one way and another. My speech in the H. of L. went off quite well : I had the unusual compliment, an audience (such an audience !) of 100 peers.

I went to the christening of Anne's little Paul at St. Margaret's, and yesterday we had Mrs. Botha, whom I had not seen for seven years, to lunch. It brought back many memories : for I shall always think that her husband was the best general of the war, and one of its wisest statesmen.

I was in the evening at a pleasant little man's dinner in Barrie's charming chambers in the Adelphi : the others (besides Barrie and myself) were Baldwin, Birrell, and Donald Maclean. There is something disarming about Baldwin, and he has besides plenty of reading a pretty sense of humour. I have been elected by the City Council High Steward of Oxford ! It involves no duties, but you must come on May 2nd, to see me introduced to the City Fathers.

I am reading Ludwig's book on the Kaiser, and about to begin *Jew Süss*—which I am not sure I shall appreciate.

SANDWICH,

22nd June, 1927.

I was delighted to get your letter this morning. Of course I had not forgotten Bertha Vibart—who could ! I leave here for The Wharf on Saturday morning next and shall be home by dinner-time that evening, when I hope I shall see you. I shall have been here just a fortnight, and despite the winds which have blown every day, I have made distinct progress in the faculty of locomotion. We have had a few visitors—Bluey, Evan Charteris, the Ormsby-Gores, and Jack and May Tennant. Barrie came over for a few hours on Sunday with Cynthia and her boy Simon. On the whole I have been leading a godly, righteous, sober and uneventful life—my main business has been the unearthing and deciphering of my old letters to you, which have revived many memories. They will afford some welcome new material for the book.

All love and blessings.

GLENCONNER,

NORTH BERWICK,

13th September, 1927.

Thank you so much for your two dear letters. I fear you had a rather hectic visit to London, but I am glad that Donovan was encouraging. " Forty winters " ! what will you say when you have to look back upon over seventy ?

We made a good journey here and found a merry lot of young people—Puff, Cys and Anne, the two " Aunts," Jack McDougall, Phyllis Spender Clay, etc., etc. Marguerite and her Geoffrey arrived last night. Puff has now gone back to his work in London.

The weather is on the whole kindly with a good allowance of sun. The air is no doubt good and has so invigorated Margot that yesterday she played 18 holes of golf at Muirfield, which is a long and rather exacting course. I have not adventured yet, tho' I think my powers of locomotion are developing. We drove over to Glen (about 40 miles) on Sunday and picnicked in the open.

I shall stay on for some time. I suppose you are on the verge of finishing the " holidays."

I *long* to see you,

H.

GLENCONNER,

NORTH BERWICK,

25th September, 1927.

I was delighted to get your last letter. I suppose you are not altogether sorry that the long holidays have come to an end.

Life here is spoiled by the persistence of execrable weather. I work in a more or less desultory fashion at my book in the mornings, and generally manage to get an afternoon drive. Rachel MacCarthy is our latest visitor : she is a very nice intelligent girl.

We went on Friday to lunch with the Balfours at Whittingehame—a few miles from here. A. J. B. is in wonderful form—in his 80th year, with no infirmities except slight deafness, and still a keen player at lawn tennis. Margot goes to London on Wednesday for a week or ten days.

197

I don't think I shall take to Katherine Mansfield. I am reading in snippets Spender's Autobiography, which is quite well done, and I shall now get hold of Ludwig's *Bismarck*, which I see is just out. He sent me a translation which he has just made of Shakespeare's sonnets.

I am distinctly more mobile. I shall move southwards early in October, staying *en route* at Castle Howard, as I am going to York on the 19th to receive the Freedom. I shall then come on to The Wharf.

GLENCONNER,

NORTH BERWICK,

2nd October, 1927.

It was a delight to get your letter, the more so as I am more or less marooned, and the weather is unspeakably damnable.

So you have finished *Napoleon* : I knew it would interest you, though I agree that the last phase makes one blush for one's country and its allies. I have a certain sympathy, all the same, with the boor Hudson Lowe. You must always remember that Napoleon had escaped from Elba, and at Waterloo had shown himself capable of being within an ace of establishing his autocracy, so to be his gaoler was no sinecure. Still it is a loathsome story.

All the young women have deserted me : Nancy, Katherine, Rachel MacCarthy, Julien Morrell : the two little aunts are with Margot and Puff at Bedford Square. Did you chance a couple of nights ago to hear Puffin on the wireless ? It was, I thought, quite good. I shall be here for another ten days or so. I don't suppose conditions are any better further south. I go to Castle Howard on about the 17th and shall be back at The Wharf on the 20th.

GLENCONNER,

NORTH BERWICK,

7th October, 1927.

Thank you so much for your letter. We have at last hit upon a spell of fine, seemingly settled weather, which makes a huge difference to the comfort of living. On the other hand, we are deserted by what you call " Youth and Beauty."

My mamma-in-law, Marguerite, played a foursome a couple of days ago, in which the other combatants were Mrs. Sassoon (aged 75), Mrs. Leo Rothschild (aged about 68), and the Dowager Lady Wemyss (some way on in the 60s) : an intrepid quartet of veterans to sally forth on a windy afternoon after about forty minutes of pouring rain. I have discovered some lovely drives within easy motoring distance.

I shall go on at the end of next week to Castle Howard, where Margot will join me, and after the function at York on Wednesday the 19th, we shall drive on Thursday to The Wharf. It will be a great joy to see you once again.

If you are still in the *Napoleon* vein, I should eschew Rosebery's *The Last Phase* (which is rather a tiresome book) and have a try at Madame de Rémusat, or Bourrienne : even if (as is probable) you have read them before. I had not heard before of " Aloysius Horn " : what sort of a fellow does he turn out to be on closer acquaintance ? I have come quite to the end of the little stock of books with which I had provided myself ; and have been reduced to reading the new volume of John Fortescue's *History of the British Army* (all about the Afghan Campaign of 1840–41— a tragic tale of perverse British blundering and inefficiency), and *Animal Mind* by a female naturalist by the name of Pitt, which has some good stuff about the habits of birds and beasts. Beb's *Young Orland* is quite amongst the best sellers : it has now reached a 15th edition. It is impossible to forecast the public taste : I should have said that his previous book— *Wind's End*—was decidedly the better of the two.

Bless you.

EPILOGUE

IT will be noticed that in the letter of 25th September, Lord Oxford speaks of himself as " distinctly more mobile." Early in the year he had felt a sudden loss of power in one leg. It was only momentary, but the weakness returned, and for some time he was condemned to a wheeled chair. Then he seemed to recover, though he still experienced some difficulty in walking, especially in mounting stairs. None of the other symptoms of a stroke was present. The improvement which he noted here, writing from North Berwick, was not maintained, though he was not noticeably worse during his stay at Castle Howard, nor on his return to The Wharf. But later, after a visit to Norfolk, he found himself unable to get out of his car, and he was never again able to go upstairs to his own room. He took to his bed, and though he was often completely himself and would take pleasure in seeing those he loved, at other times he lived in a dream ; his intellect unimpaired but his sense of his surroundings confused. He died on 15th February, 1928.

D. M.

INDEX

Abbey Theatre, Dublin, 165
Abbotsbury, 180
Aberdeen, Marchioness of, 124
Aberdeen, Marquess of, 124
Abingdon, 42, 152
Abingdon Street, 59, 123, 143, 167, 171
Academy, Royal, 3, 42, 65, 169, 188
Adam in Moonshine, 188
Adam's Breed, 191
Adams, Bridges, 63
Addison, 25
Æschylus, 18
Aga Khan, the, 64, 72, 132
Ainley, Henry, 156, 192
Alba, Duke and Duchess of, 78
Albanesi, Meggie, 31
Alcestis, the, 21
Alderley, 86, 88–9
Alexandra, Queen, 146–7
Allgood, Sarah, 192
Ambassadors, Conference of, 73
America, *see* United States
Anatolia, 34
Animal Mind, 200
Anna Christie, 52
" Anne," *see* Asquith
Antigone, the, 6–8, 72
" Antoine," *see* Bibesco
Antony and Cleopatra, 44
Anyhouse, 127
Aristophanes, 166
Armistice Day, 145
Arnold, Matthew, 137
Ashmolean Museum, 67
Asia Minor, 34
Asquith, Anne (Mrs. Cyril), 194, 196
Asquith, Anthony (" Puffin "), 34–5, 52–4, 66, 68, 81, 103, 127, 130, 142–3, 154–5, 157, 164, 169–70, 179, 196, 199
Asquith, Brig.-Gen. Arthur (" Oc "), 7, 107, 113, 115, 117
Asquith, Mrs. Arthur (" Betty "), 77

Asquith, Lady Cynthia (" Cynthia "), 57
Asquith, Cyril (" Cys "), 72, 119, 144, 196
Asquith, Herbert (" Beb "), 77, 119, 200
Asquith, Mrs. Herbert, 77
Asquith, Mrs. (" Margot " ; later Countess of Oxford), xi, 1, 5, 7, 19, 21, 34, 46, 52, 57, 64, 66, 68, 78–9, 83–5, 89, 96, 103, 122, 127, 134–5, 142–3, 172, 193, 196
Asquith, Raymond, ix
Asquith wigs, 14, 16
Assouan, 113–16
Astor, Lady, 44
Ault, Marie, 31
Austen, Jane, 5
Australia, 5, 33, 185
Aylmer, Felix, 126

Baalbec, 112
Babbitt, 40
Bad Man, The, 47
Bailey, Sir Abe, 173
Baker, Harold, 180
Baldwin, Stanley, 61, 80, 82, 90, 113, 123, 166, 184, 194
Balfour, Earl, 5, 79, 123, 125, 197
Ballin, 14, 32
Balliol College, 9, 32, 136–7
Bank of England, 57, 59, 122
Barakat, 117
Baring, Hon. Maurice, 63
Barnes, Kenneth, 158
Barrie, Sir James, 119, 194–5
Barrymore, John, 125, 160
Beasts, Men and Gods, 59
Beau Geste, 125
Beauchamp, Countess, 154
Beauchamp, Earl, 123, 154
Beaverbrook, Lord, 78–9
" Beb," *see* Asquith
Beechman, Mr., 13, 15–16
Beerbohm, Max, 62

INDEX

Belinda, 11
Bell, Henry, 93
Bell, Sir Hugh, 89
Benn, Wedgwood, 84
Bennett, Arnold, 34, 103
Beresford, Jack, 127
Berlin, 46, 149, 184
Berry, Anita, 186
Best, Edna, 193
Bethmann-Hollweg, 28, 32, 73
" Betty," *see* Asquith
Between Time and Tweed, 71
Beyrout, 110
Bibesco, Prince Antoine (" Antoine "), 37, 39, 108–9, 153
Bibesco, Princess Elizabeth (" Elizabeth "), 25, 39, 42, 77, 93, 108, 125–6, 136, 154, 157, 164, 176, 179
Bibesco, Princess Marthe, 108–9
Biggar, Mr., 82, 84, 90
Birkenhead, Earl (" F. E. Smith "), 133, 152, 160
Birmingham, George A., 180
Birmingham Repertory Company, 148
Birrell, Augustine, 120, 133, 171, 194
Birth control, 168
Bismarck, 19, 20, 34
Bismarck, Ludwig's, 198
Black Pirate, The, 160
Blackwell, E., 7
Blackwell (Oxford), 74
Bloomsbury, 161
Bluebeard's Eighth Wife, 20
Boar's Hill, xi, 65, 68
Bolshevik banners, 88–9
Bonar Law, 9, 38, 40, 61, 79, 82
" Bongie," *see* Bonham-Carter
Bonham-Carter, Sir Maurice (" Bongie "), 6, 28, 125, 132
Bonham-Carter, Lady (" Violet "), 6, 7, 28, 42, 57, 71, 83–4
Boswell, 39, 46, 118
Botha, Gen., 194
Botha, Mrs. 194
Boucher, 67
Bourne, Cardinal, 166
Bournemouth, 53–4, 99
Bourrienne, 200
Bowood, 41
Boyd, Phyllis, 165
Bradfield, 7, 8
Bradford, Lady, 60
Brazil, 165
Breadalbane, Marchioness of, 135

Bretherton, Mr., 113
Briand, Aristide, 149
Bridgeman, W. C. (later Viscount Bridgeman), 61
Bridges, Dr. Robert, 30
British Museum, 55, 175, 177
Broadway, 187
Broughton, Rhoda, 124
Brown, Mr., 82
Browning, Robert, 91, 123, 128
Buchan, John, 17
Buckingham Palace, 47, 51, 103
Buckle, George, 98
Buckmaster, Lady, 142
Buckmaster, Lord, 41, 53, 90, 127, 168, 175
Bumpus's, 186
Burke, 46
Burlington House, 78, 92
Burnand, Sir Frank, 25
Buxton, 63

Cadell, Jean, 104
Cairo, 113
Cambridge, 48–9, 70, 142
Cambridge History, 53
Campbell, Miss, 153
Campbell-Bannerman, Sir H., 19
Canada, 43, 184
Cannes, 188
Canterbury, Archbishop of, 97, 133
Capablanca, 14
Cape Horn, 33
Cape of Good Hope, 33
Capel, Diana, 5
Capel Sion, 46
Capernaum, 111
Caprivi, 19, 35
Cardiff, 94
Carducci, 10
Carline, Richard, 51
Carline, Sydney, 42, 51–2, 64
Carlyle, 39
Carmichael, 177
Carnarvon, 171
Carson, Lord, 79
Cassel, Sir Ernest, 66
Cassell and Co., vii, 21, 38, 74
Castle Howard, 153, 198–201
Castle of Otranto, 61
Cat's Cradle, 166
Cave, Edward, 38
Cave, Viscount, 133, 136–7
Cecil, Lord David, 138
Cecil, Lord Hugh, 56, 75

INDEX

Cecil, Lord Robert (later Visc. Cecil), 8, 9, 75, 135
Cellier, 126
Cézanne, 68, 109
Chantrey Trustees, 2
Chaplin, Charlie, 154
Charlotte, Queen, 77
Charteris, Hon. Evan, 195
Charteris, Frances, 144
Chekov, 23, 143, 158, 186
Chelsea Flower Show, 63
Cherry Orchard, The, 134
Chesterton, G. K., 2
Christie's, 67
Churchill, Lady Gwendoline, 120, 167
Churchill, Winston, 8, 9, 37, 53, 80–1, 123, 139, 160, 193
Churchill, Mrs. Winston, 160, 191
Cincinnati, 1
Clarendon Press, 147
Classical Association, the, 162
Clay, Phyllis Spender, 196
Clifford, Dr., 104
Clynes, J. R., 53
Coalition Government, the, 36
Coalition Liberals, 39, 44
Coats' Memorial Church, 85
Coleridge, 38
Collier, Mary, 17
Collins, Sir Godfrey, 132, 173
Communists, the, 82, 84, 88
Congreve, 96
Connard, Philip, 4
Conservatives, the, 9, 90, 106
Constant Nymph, The, 110, 120, 192
Constantine, King, 34
Cooper, Lady Diana Duff, 126, 167
Cooper, Gladys, 6, 57
Corelli, Marie, 2, 100
Corfu, 73, 76
Cormack, 82, 84, 90
Corot, 83
Corporation of London, 102
Cosimo, Piero di, 67
Cossacks, the, 140
Courtauld, S., 175
Coward, Noel, 125, 178
Cowdray, Lady, 4
Cowdray, Lord, 8
Cowl, Jane, 178
Crawfurd, Maj. Horace, 92
Crewe, Marquess of, 8, 41, 93, 125
Cunard, Lady, 57
Curzon, Hon. Frank, 130

Curzon, Marquess, 128–30
Cust, Harry, 110
Cust, Mr., 110
Cyclops, the, 70
" Cynthia," see Asquith
" Cys," see Asquith

D'Abernon, Lady, 46
D'Abernon, Lord, 46, 149, 175, 184
Daily News, 162
Daily Telegraph, 139
Dalmatia, 131
Damascus, 111–12
Damsel in Distress, A, 91
Dante, 1
Darwin, 155
Davidson, Mrs., 102
Dawson, Geoffrey, 163
Dawson's stables, 72
Dear Brutus, 146
Death, Lord Oxford's, xii, 201
Degas, 68, 175
Demosthenes, 72
Derby, the, 64–5, 132, 173
Derenburgs, the, 35
Dewsbury, 79
Dictatorships, 170
Dictionary of National Biography, 43
Diehards, the, 9
Dilly, the bookseller, 39
Disraeli, 94, 98, 101, 155
Disraeli, Mrs., 98
" Dobbie," see Dobson
Dobson, Frank (" Dobbie "), 47, 51, 58, 93–4, 128
Dolls' House, the Queen's, 24, 30, 47
Doll's House, Ibsen's, 149
" Dominie," the, see Sampson
Donaldson, Canon, 146
D'Orsay, Count, 101
Dostoievsky, 56
Dr. Thorne, 124
Dragons, the, 108
Drummond, Sir Eric, 7, 22
Du Maurier, Gerald, 62, 104–5, 192
Dublin, 165
Dudley, Earl of, 74
Duff, Lady Juliet, 138
Duranti, Mons., 175
Duse, Eleonora, 100

Eadie, Dennis, 104
East of Suez, 31
Easy Virtue, 178
Edinburgh, 162–3, 165

INDEX

Egypt, 107–8, 113, 115, 155
Elba, 198
Elder Brethren, the, 140
Election results, 90, 106–7
" Elizabeth," *see* Bibesco
Elizabeth, Queen, 166–7
Emmott, Lord, 186
Ems, 99
Epsom, 64
Epstein, 176
Eugenics and Other Evils, 2
Euripides, 91
Evans, Caradoc, 46
Evans, Edith, 96, 125–6
Evening Standard, 181
Eviction Bill, 100
Eze, 189

Faber, Col., 65
Faber, Leslie, 103
Fagan, Mr., 146, 148
Fairbanks, Douglas, 154, 157, 160
Farringdon, 74
Fielding, Henry, 75
Fiery Particles, 43
Flemish Exhibition, 188
Flower, Mr., 38
Fontainebleau, 42
Forbes-Robertson, Jean, 158
Forbes-Robertson, Lady, 157
Forbes-Robertson, Sir Johnston, 95, 157–8
Fortescue, Hon. John, 200
France, 55, 93, 101
Franklin, Miss, 42
Frederick, Pauline, 155, 192
French Revolution, 83, 149–50
French Revolution, Carlyle's, 39
Freyberg, Col., 6
Futility, 18, 23

Gainsborough, 65, 67, 137
Galilee, 111
Gandhi, 16
Garda, Lago di, 110
Gardiner, A. G., 64
Garrick, 46
Garrick Club, 10
Gates, Mr., 77
Gay Lord Quex, 55
General Elections, 36, 90
General Strike, the, x, 168–70, 172
Genesis of the War, 21, 72, 74
Geneva, 7, 20, 164–5, 179
Genoa, 9

Gentlemen of China, 94
George III, King, 77
George V, King, 35, 47, 51, 69, 108, 123–4
George Eliot, 193
George, Lloyd, *see* Lloyd
Gerhardi, William, 19
Germany, 34, 165
Gezirah dam, 117
Ghirlandaio, 67
Ghost Train, The, 155–6
Giannini, 103
Gibbon, 31, 159
Gish, Lilian, 155, 192
Gladstone, 5, 32, 155, 159
Gladstone and Disraeli, 155
Gladstone, Viscount, 8, 37
Glasgow, 84–6, 89, 90, 106, 162–3
Glastonbury, 21
Godley, Hugh, 31
Goldsmith, 25, 65
Gore, Bishop, 5, 138
Gosse, Sir Edmund, 165
Grant, Duncan, 70
Grant, Sir Hamilton, 24, 28
Graves, Nancy, 10
Graves, Robert, 10
Graves, Walter, 2, 3
Gray, Frank, 16, 44
Great Adventure, 103
Greece, 33–4, 73, 76, 120, 131
Green Goddess, The, 78, 103
Greenock, 182
Greenwood, Sir Hamar, 37
Gregory, Lady, 165
Grey, Lady Jane, 166
Grey, Viscount, 8, 9, 16, 59, 68, 107, 123, 140, 152, 171, 181, 186
Grillion's, 95, 163
Grundy, Mr., 135
Guedalla, Philip, 15–16, 64
Guest, Capt. the Hon. F., 37
Guildhall, 102, 175
Gull, Sir W., 99

Haggard, Sir Rider, 179
Haldane, Elizabeth, 193
Haldane, J. B. S., 49
Haldane, Lord, 5, 28, 193
Halicarnassus, 68, 86
Hamilton, Cicely, 148
Hamlet, 94
Hartley, Leslie, 35, 103
Harvard, 148
Harvey, Gert, 26

INDEX

Haselden, 157
" Hawthornden " Prize, 162, 165
Hazlitt, 118
Hemans, Mrs., 186
Henderson, H. D., 49, 60
Heneage, Mrs., 155, 180
Henry VIII, 166
Henson, Bishop of Durham, 119
Herbert, Basil, 14–15, 56, 89, 133
Hermon, Mount, 112
Hertzog, Gen., 185
Hewart, Lord, 131
Higgins, Mr., 127
Hindenburg, 132
History of England, Trevelyan's, 179
History of the British Army, Fortescue's, 200
Hogarth, 122
Hogg, Douglas (later Lord Hailsham), 40, 160
Hogge, J. M., 39
Holdens, the, 28
Holman, Miss, 189
Homer, 166
Hope, Anthony, 179
Hoppner, 67, 83
Horace, 118
Horn, Aloysius, 200
Horne, Sir Robert, 160
Horner, Lady, 43
House, Col., 28–9, 32, 140
House of Commons, 6, 37, 39, 108
House of Lords, 9, 125, 128–31, 138, 152, 164–5, 168, 194
Howard, Hon. Geoffrey, 37, 135
Hudson, Sir Robert, 37
Hunt, American journalist, 4
Huntingtower, 17, 23

Ibsen, 23, 83, 140
If Winter Comes, 5
In Dark Places, 82
Inchcape, Lord, 60
Independents, the, 90
India, 32, 78
Inge, Dean, 145, 151, 166
Intrigues of the War, 13
Ireland, 5, 8, 9, 50
Isaacs, Sir R., *see* Reading
Isham, Gyles, 94
Italian poetry, 1
Italy, 73, 76

Jansi, Comte de, 165
Japan, 73

Jenner, Sir W., 99
Jerusalem, 110–11
Jesse, Miss Tennyson, 127
Jew Süss, 193–4
John, Augustus, 11, 93–4, 176
John, Gwen, 176
John Bull, 6
Johnson, Dr., 38–9, 46, 75–6, 117–18
Johnstone, Harcourt, 46
Jones, Robert, 184
Jowitt, Sir W., 50
Joynson-Hicks, Sir W. (later Lord Brentford), 113
Judæa, 111
Jumbo, 1
Juno and the Paycock, 163–4
Just Married, 122

Kaiser, the, 14, 16–17, 19, 21, 25–6, 28, 31–2, 34–5, 102, 194
" Katherine," *see* Tennant
Keeble, Sir F. and Lady, 20
Kellaway, F. G., 37
Kendal, Mrs., 119
Kenyon, Sir Frederick, 5
Keppel, Mrs., 121
Kettle, Tilly, 120
Keynes, J. M., 10, 14, 49, 70–1
Keys, Nelson, 192
Khartoum, 115, 117
Kidd, Dr., 99
Kilbracken, Lord, 31–2
King, Mackenzie, 184
King's College, Cambridge, 70
King's College, London, 159
Kipling, 83
Kitchener, 116
Kneller, 118
Knight, H., 169
Krassin, 59

Labourites, the, 86
Labour Government, the, 95, 106
Labour Party, the, 90
Lamb, Henry, 76
Lamourette, le baiser de, 39, 83
Landi, Elissa, 193
Lane, Sir Arbuthnot, 151
Lane, John, 46, 120
Lansdowne, Marquess of, 40
Lascelles, Frank, 189
Lavery, Sir John, 42
Law, Bonar, *see* Bonar
League of Nations, 7, 20, 29, 73, 165, 179

INDEX

Leverhulme, Lord, 51
Lewis, Sinclair, 46
Liberal and Radical Candidates'
   Association, 173
Liberal Fair, the, 150
Liberal " Million " Fund, 132
Liberal Party, the, 106, 172–4, 182
Liberal Summer Schools, the, 14,
   70–1, 142
Lincoln's Inn, 131
Lincolnshire, Marquess of, 133
Lindsay, A. D., 119
Lindsay, Ronald, 25, 77, 184
Liverpool, 149–50
Lloyd George, D., 9, 17, 39, 54, 59,
   83, 85, 104, 107, 123, 141, 167,
   171–4, 176, 178, 186
Lloyd George, Dame Margaret, 150
Lloyd George, Megan, 84–5
Locarno Pact, 149, 165
Lombardy, 110
London, 59, 81, 102, 113, 168
London Hospital, 103
Longworth, Mrs., 68
Lonsdale, Earl of, 47
Lopokova, 143
Loraine, Robert, 96
Lowe, Sir Hudson, 198
Lowther, Arthur, 154
Loyalties, 11
" Lucy," see Smith
Ludwig, Emil, 194, 198
Luxor, 113–16
Lyall, Sir Alfred, 32
Lynd, Robert, 17

MacCarthy, Desmond, xii, 38, 126,
   141, 158, 171, 187
MacCarthy, Rachel, 183, 197, 199
MacDonald, J. Ramsay, 53, 90, 95,
   104, 106, 146
MacDougal, Jack, 35, 196
MacEvoy, 4
Mackail, J. W., 141
McKenna, Reginald, 11
McKinnell, Norman, 20
McLaren, Barbara, 6
McLaren, Hon. H. D., 37
Maclay, Lord, 85
Maclean, Sir Donald, 8, 15–17, 37–8,
   107, 194
Madras House, 149
Magda, 57
Major Barbara, 6
Manchester, 54, 86, 88–9

Manet, 68, 120
Mansfield, Katherine, 198
Mansfield, Lord, 76
Marchant, Mr., 119, 128, 143, 145
" Margot," see Asquith
Marie Louise of Schleswig-Holstein,
   Princess, 24
Marionettes, the, 53–4
Marjoribanks, Edward, 41
Mary, Princess, 47, 51, 53
Mary, Queen, 24, 47, 51, 69
Mary Queen of Scots, 167
Masefield, John (" Jan "), 2, 11, 31,
   69
Master Builder, The, 83
Masterman, C. F. G. and Mrs., 11
Maule, Sir R., 164
Maurice, Gen., 11, 13
Meiklejohn, Sir Roderick, 75, 92
Meistersänger, The, 134
Melloney Holstpur, 69
Memling, 188
Memories and Reflections, vii, xi
Meredith, George, 25
Mesopotamia, 44
Metternich, 74
Metternich, Count, 66
Mill Hill School, 139
Milne, A. A., 47
Mitchell, E. R., 106
Moby Dick, 160
Monaco, 190
Mond, Sir Alfred, 112
Mont Agel, 191
Montagu, Edwin, 37, 78
Montagu, Mrs., 18
Montague, C. E., 43
Monte Carlo, 99
More, Hannah, 151
Morgan, Cope, 15, 17, 71
Morley, John, 19
Morrell, Julien, 199
Mosley, Sir O., 61
Mrs. Beam, 104
Mudge, Prebendary, 118
Muir, Ramsay, 159
Mumtaz Mahal, 72, 76
Munnings, A. J., 11
Murray, Agnes, 12, 20
Murray, Gilbert, 12, 20–1, 58, 159
Murray, Lady Mary, 12, 20
Mussolini, 73, 75, 110

Nablus, 111
Napoleon, 27, 74

INDEX

Napoleon, 198, 200
Nash, John, 128
Nash, Paul, 52,
Nathan, Sir Matthew, 180
Nation, The, 49, 60
National Arts Collection Fund, 175
National Gallery, 120
National Liberal Club, 38, 90, 133
National Liberal Federation, 59, 174
Nazareth, 111–12
New Arabian Nights, 143
New College, 69
New English Arts Club, 64
New Statesman, The, 4, 17
New Zealand, 33, 185
Nicholas, Tsar, 47
Nicholson, Benjamin, 62
Nicholson, William, 48, 62, 128, 145
Nicholson, Winifred, 62
Nile, the, 115
Nisbett, Cathleen, 193
Notre-Dame, 109
Nottingham, 86–7

Oaks, the, 64
" Oc," *see* Asquith
O'Casey, Sean, 162, 164–5
O'Connor, T. P., 43, 59, 163
Old Adam, The, 148
Olympia, 139
O'Neill, Eugene, 45, 52
Opie, 67
Oresteia, the, 70
Orissers, The, 59
Ormsby-Gore, W. G. A., 195
Orpen, Sir W., 24, 92, 145, 152, 169
Osiris, 114
Ovid, 166
Oxford, 13–14, 16, 18, 24, 44, 49, 53, 68, 133, 139, 184, 194
Oxford, Bishop of, 166
Oxford Book of Italian Verse, 1
Oxford Chancellorship, the, 133
Oxford, Countess of, *see* Asquith
Oxford Union, the, 41, 184
Oxford University Liberal Club, 24

Paderewski, 141
Padua, 64
Page Memorial, the, 68
Painted Swan, The, 126–8
Paisley, 9, 36, 64, 82–4, 86, 88, 90–1, 106, 182
Palestine, 112

Paris, 6, 7, 55, 93, 108–10, 180
Parker, Sir Gilbert, 189
Parsons, Viola, 11, 34, 55, 126, 142
Party meetings, 41, 44, 50, 54, 65
Paulton, Harry, 21, 34, 42
Pavement, The, 82
Peerage, offer of a, 108
Pekin, 26
Petrouska, 143
Philæ, 115
Phillipps, Vivian, 16, 24, 132
Phillips, Mrs., 139
Philpot, Glyn, 57
Pickford, Mary, 154, 157
Pindar, 18
Pinero, Sir Arthur, 55
Pitt, Frances, 200
Pitt, William, 6
Plato, 81
Playboy of the Western World, The, 46
Playfair, Nigel, 34, 96
Poland, 165
Pope, Muriel, 128
Poplar, 95
Portugal, Queen of, 94
Post-Impressionists, the, 109
Priestley, J. B., 188
Primitives, the English, 78
Princess Ida, 185
Pringle, W. M. R., 10, 58
Procter, Mrs., 169
Provence, 129, 190
Pryde, James, 2, 4, 145
" Puffin," *see* Asquith
Punch, 163

Quiller-Couch, Sir A., 80

Raeburn, 177
Raleigh, Sir W., 158, 189
Rameses II, 114
Rathbone, H. R., 149
Rea, Isabella, 14–15, 56
Reading, Marquess of, 16, 140, 175
Rector's Daughter, The, 119, 121
Rémusat, Mme de, 200
Reynolds, Sir Joshua, 65, 67, 83, 118, 137
Ribblesdale, Lady, 7, 72, 191
Richelieu, 30
Rin-Tin-Tin, 156
Riviera, the, 189
Roberts, Lady Cecilia, 62
Robins, Elizabeth, 83
Robinson, Crabb, 74

INDEX

Robinson, Sir J. B., 67
Rocksavage, Lady, 4
Rollitt, Sir Albert, 18
Romney, 67
Roosevelt, Theodore, 29, 32, 68-9
Ros, Amanda, 87
Rose Marie, 129
Rosebery, Earl of, 200
Rothenstein, W., 42
Rothermere, Lord, 78
Rothschild, Mrs. Leo, 199
Roxburgh and Selkirk, 24
Royal Academy, 3, 42, 65, 169, 188
Rubens, 188
Rumania, 153
Rumania, King of, 102
Rumania, Queen of, 102, 141
Runciman, Walter, 15, 17, 181
Ruskin School Appeal, 95
Russell, Hon. Charles, 57
Russell divorce case, 12
Russia, 18, 59, 88

St. Anthony, 60, 63-4
St. Francis, 64
St. John the Baptist, 111
St. Julien des Pauvres, 109
St. Louis, 1
St. Paul, 172
St. Valentine, 43
Salisbury, Marquess of, 26
Samaritans, the, 111
Sampson, Dr. John (the "Dominie"),
    12, 153
Samuel, Sir Herbert, 42
Sanders, 161
Sands, Miss, 93-4, 158
Sargent, 4
Sassoon, Mrs., 199
Scaliger, 162, 166
Schuster, Sir George and Lady, 117
Scotland, 36, 163, 182
Sea Beast, The, 160
Seabrooke, E., 52
Seagull, The, 143, 148
Seaman, Sir Owen, 163
Second Empire, The, 15
Second Mrs. Tanqueray, The, 6
Sefton Park, 80
Seurat, 172
" Shadow " Cabinet, Liberal, 171
Shakespeare, 55, 198
Sharp, Clifford, 4, 25, 55, 63
Shaw, Bernard, 56, 149
Shaw, McInnes, 84, 90

Shechem, 111
Sheffield, Earl of, 89
Sheppard, Dr. J. T., 70
Sheridan, Mary, 158
Sherrington, Sir Charles, 136
Simon, Dr. and Mrs., 161
Simon, E. D., 101
Simon, Sir John, 12-13, 15-17, 43, 53,
    57, 101, 107, 133, 173, 181
Singapore, 69, 185
Skelton, A. N., 183
Smith, F. E., *see* Birkenhead
Smith, Mrs. Graham ("Lucy"), xi,
    5, 22, 46, 151
Smyrna, 34
Snowden, Philip, 151
Soane, Sir John, 121-2
Socrates, 81, 175, 177
Somervell, Donald, 7
Somerville, David and Mrs., 155
South Wales, 141
Spain, 78, 165
Speaker, the, 50
Spectator, the, 72
Spencer, Helen, 193
Spencer, Stanley, 77, 145, 191, 193
Spender, J. A., 28, 55, 198
Spender, Mrs., 28
Spook Sonata, The, 185
Stamfordham, Lord, 106-7
Star, the, 163
Steer, Wilson, 2
Stenhouse, Ernest, 65
Stevenson, Sir Daniel, 162-3
Stevenson, Frances, 171
Stevenson, R. L., 143
Strahan, the publisher, 38
Strasbourg, 30
Stratford-on-Avon, 63, 71, 156
Strindberg, 185
Strong, Mrs., 141
Sudan, the, 116
Sudermann, 57
Sunday Times, The, 169
Susan Lennox, 23
Sutherland, Dowager Duchess of,
    18

Tacitus, 72
Tate Gallery, 175, 177
Taylor, J. H., 103
Tempest, The, 63
Tempest, Marie, 125, 166
Tennant, Sir Charles, 183
Tennant, Jack, 85, 195

INDEX

Tennant, Katherine, 77, 131, 170, 183, 199
Tennant, Marguerite, 196, 199
Tennant, May, 195
Tennant, Nan, 77, 129, 135
Tennant, Nancy, 131, 183, 199
Tenniel, Sir John, 20
Tennyson, Lionel, 5
Tennyson, Lord, 5
That Woman Business, 167
The Price She Paid, 21, 23, 27
Three Sisters, 158
Tiberias, 111–2
Times, The, 5, 6, 14, 30, 58, 74, 80, 92, 133, 144, 163–4, 169–70, 192
Tintagel, 17
Tirpitz, 28, 32
Titheradge, Madge, 20, 156
Toccata, The, 128
Tonks, Henry, 76
Tonson, Jacob, 38
Tree, Maud, 6
Tree, Viola, 11, 34, 55, 126, 142
Trevelyan, G. M., 179
Trevelyan, Hilda, 103
Turkey, 33–4, 120
Tussaud, Mme, 3
Tutankhamen, 114
Tyrrell, Sir W. (later Lord Tyrrell), 16, 22, 28, 33, 47

Ucello, 4, 22
Union, Oxford, 41, 184
Unitarians, the, 134
United States, 1, 5, 23, 25, 29, 37

Van Dyck, 65, 188
Van Eyck, 188
Vanderbilt Ball, the, 66, 68
Vanya, 158
Venezelos, 120
Venezuela, 26
Venice, 35, 73
Versailles Treaty, 29
Vibart, Bertha, 195
Victoria, Queen, 94
Victorians, the, 89
Vienna, 74
" Violet," *see* Bonham-Carter
Virgil, 166
Voltaire, 149

Vortex, The, 125
Voyage to Lisbon, 75
Vuillard, 109

Waddesdon, 136–7
Wady Halfa, 116
Wakefield, Hugh, 21
Wales, Prince of, 22, 37, 42, 79
Walkley, A. B., 126, 149
Walpole, Horace, 61
Walsall, 81
Walsh, Senator, 141
Walton, Izaak, 189
Washington Treaty, 12
Waterloo, 198
Waterloo Bridge, 175
" Watson Pasha," 116
Watt, G. Fiddes, 92
Way of the World, The, 96
Webb, Mrs. Beatrice, 159
Webb, Sidney, 159
Wells, of Wadham, 97, 139
Wembley, 103
Wesley, 91
Weymss, Lord and Lady, 167
Westminster Abbey, 68, 79, 130, 146
Westminster Chapel, 104
Westminster Hall, 38, 69
Wharton, Edith, 46
Whatcombe, 72, 161
Wild Duck, The, 140
Wilkes, 39
Willmot, Miss, 63
Wilson, President, 28–30
Wilson, Steuart, 21
Wimborne, Lady, 105
Wind's End, 200
Windsor, 48
Wodehouse, P. G., 74, 88, 91
Women's Liberal Federation, 57
Wordsworth, 155
Workers' Weekly, 106
World Crisis, The, 53
Worthington-Evans, Sir L., 113

Yearsley, Ann, 18
York, 198, 200
York, Duke and Duchess of, 50
Young Orland, 200
Young Visiters, The, 61